SCULPTING DATA FOR ML

The first act of Machine Learning

Jigyasa Grover & Rishabh Misra

Sculpting Data for ML

First Edition

First published in January 2021.

ISBN 979-8-585-46357-0

Library of Congress Control Number: 2020921199

Cover photo by Nick Bondarev from Pexels.

We dedicate this book to dear Almighty and our beloved families for their unwavering support in all our personal and professional endeavors.

"The real voyage of discovery consists not in seeking new landscapes, but in having new eyes."

- Marcel Proust

FOREWORD
By Julian McAuley

Many recent breakthroughs in Machine Learning, including Natural Language Processing, Computer Vision, etc. owe as much to having better *data* as they owe to having better models.

Naturally, modern ML datasets should be *large*, in order for models to capture their complex underlying semantics. However having enough data is only a small part of the problem: data must also be processed, appropriately represented, properly sampled, freed from issues of balance and bias etc., not to mention the challenge of extracting meaningful predictive information.

A common experience among ML practitioners is that this type of "data munging" occupies more time and effort than modeling; it is also incredibly rewarding, as the collection and curation of new datasets often facilitates the most novel and exciting research, and can represent a significant contribution to the research community.

It is wonderful to see a book that covers the underexplored but important skill of collecting and curating data. I expect this will be useful to practitioners who are beginning to collect their own datasets, or wondering how popular datasets are typically collected. Such topics are typically missing from academic treatment of machine learning, where the massive task of data collection and preparation is so often glossed over.

I was thrilled to hear Jigyasa and Rishabh were working on this book: both have experience collecting, curating, and modeling large datasets, both in academic and industrial settings. I expect readers will find the sections on data extraction and data preparation especially useful, as these are the skills I have found most useful in my own career.

Julian McAuley
Associate Professor, University of California San Diego

FOREWORD
By Laurence Moroney

This is an important book!

Data is the lifeblood of any Machine Learning or AI solution, and there is only so far you can go with publicly available datasets. What excites me about this book is that Jigyasa and Rishabh go beyond these, and teach you how to create, curate, and manage data effectively.

They will take you through a number of scenarios where they got real-world data from varied sources like online retail and news aggregator websites, but, instead of a rough copy-and-paste, they will instead demonstrate the pipeline involved in making the dataset eminently usable.

Chapter 3 of this book is especially powerful, where you'll see how, from first principles, to go through the processes of data trimming, anonymization, standardization, transformation, and balancing. Chapter 4 will take you through the important task of feature engineering, where, instead of just throwing raw data at the problem, you can refine and improve it with clipping, scaling, bucketization, and a lot more.

All of this will prepare you for Machine Learning with your own custom data that you have sourced, cleaned, and managed for optimal model creation.

I am really excited by this field, and delighted that a book like this one exists. Pick it up, read, learn, enjoy!

Laurence Moroney
Lead Artificial Intelligence Advocate, Google

FOREWORD
By Mengting Wan

Throughout the rapid growth of Machine Learning and Data Science these years, data is always the key foundation for almost any downstream research, analysis, or intelligent product feature development. One may easily notice that numerous books and courses exist nowadays about helping people manage the skills of consuming the data; however, there are very few resources talking about how to carefully collect, process, and curate high quality datasets. I used to work with Rishabh Misra on several research projects at UC San Diego and have learned many practical data collection and processing skills from him. Therefore I am so excited to hear that Jigyasa and Rishabh are willing to share their knowledge in this domain, and really appreciate their efforts on this book.

The book introduces critical data collection, extraction, preparation, and processing skills. It also provides several Machine Learning application examples and approaches the data problems from the application-oriented perspective. I personally find this book can be very helpful for researchers and practitioners, in order to remove their data availability obstacles, help them proactively but responsibly gather the data they need, and understand the strengths as well as limitations of their datasets. In this regard, I think the book will be ideal as a starting point for data enthusiasts who are willing to learn the dataset collection process from scratch.

Mengting Wan
Senior Applied Scientist, Microsoft

PREFACE

In the contemporary world of Artificial Intelligence and Machine Learning, *data is the new oil*. Rightly so, giant leaps in this domain can be attributed to access to large-scale data. Despite this fact, most of the focus often lies in the methodological aspect of Machine Learning, which is excellent for a start but can limit our advancement. Upon reaching a certain comfort level with modish methodologies, only tackling problems for which a well-prepared dataset is already available curbs our potential. Hence, for Machine Learning algorithms to work their magic, it is imperative to lay a firm foundation by acquiring knowledge of curating good quality datasets.

With the modern bloom of social networks, online retailers, streaming platforms, and knowledge and experience sharing platforms, there is no shortage of any form of data, be it textual, audio, or visual. Therefore, an extensive amount of crude data is available at our fingertips. All we need are the skills to identify valuable information and extract meaningful datasets to fashion more precise models.

Sculpting Data for ML functions as the first act of the play of Machine Learning. It aims at enlightening Machine Learning and Artificial Intelligence enthusiasts, practitioners, and data scientists about one of the fundamental aspects of this realm, *Dataset Curation*. This stage often does not get its due limelight yet has high relevance in both Academia and Industry. This book's distinctive feature is that it puts forward a step-by-step guide on constructing a good quality dataset from scratch. The hands-on tutorial ingrained in the book uses Python with tools like BeautifulSoup and Selenium to coach how to ethically gather data from various web sources. The whole flow is pinned on the fact that predictive models necessitate access to relevant, structured, and distinctive data to maneuver effectively.

Overall, the book covers different techniques for dataset building, preprocessing, and engineering impactful features, thus highlighting the significance of data representation for Machine Learning models. Apart from molding data in its worthy format, this book also discusses ways to deal with noisy and unreliable data. Towards the end, it lays out various Machine Learning paradigms, and their data needs to showcase how to identify suitable learning algorithms to solve challenging problems effectively.

This book invites readers to traverse through the pragmatic journey of dataset curation. The goal is to institute the significance of data, especially in its worthy format, and recognize its effect on advancing Machine Learning systems' capability.

Jigyasa Grover & Rishabh Misra

TABLE OF CONTENTS

FOREWORD BY JULIAN MCAULEY　　　　　ix

FOREWORD BY LAURENCE MORONEY　　　　xi

FOREWORD BY MENGTING WAN　　　　　xiii

PREFACE　　　　　xv

CHAPTER 1: INTRODUCTION　　　　　1

The Modern Bloom　　　　　1
Significance Of Data　　　　　3
Honing Dataset Curation Skills　　　　　5
　Importance in Academia　　　　　6
　Importance in Industry　　　　　7

What Will This Book Teach?   7

CHAPTER 2: DATASET EXTRACTION   11

The Planning Phase   11
  Where is the Data? Overview of the Data Sources   12
  Sample Datasets   12
  Situational Analysis   14
    Guided Search   14
      Challenge   14
      Relevant Data Identification 14
    Unguided Search   18
      Challenge   19
      General Data Search   19
The Extraction Phase   22
  Toolkit Overview   22
    Chrome and Chrome Driver   22
    Beautiful Soup   23
    Selenium   27
  Basic Rules   27
  Step-By-Step Process   28
    Structure Understanding of the data source 28
    Static & Dynamic Content Extraction   31
    Key Information Acquisition   32
      Product Links' Extraction   32
      Product Reviews' Extraction 36
    Process Automation   40
    Error Handling   44
    Request Rate Limitations   47
  Expected Outcome   49

CHAPTER 3: DATASET PREPARATION 53

Data Trimming 53
Data Anonymization 60
Data Standardization 63
Data Integration 67
    Vertical Integration 67
    Horizontal Integration 69
Data Transformation 70
Data Balancing 73
    Eliminating Infrequent Data Records 74
    Randomly Sampling Data Records 75
    Assigning Class Weights 76
    Picking Correct Evaluation Metric 77
    Alter Problem Definition 78
Data Exporting 79

CHAPTER 4: DATASET PREPROCESSING & FEATURE ENGINEERING 85

Data Preprocessing 86
Vectorization 86
    Text Vectorization 87
    Image Vectorization 90
    Categorical Vectorization 92
        Integer Encoding 92
        One-Hot Encoding 93
Normalization 94
    Feature Clipping 95
    Range Scaling 96
    Log Scaling 96

Z-Score Scaling 97

Bucketization 98

Symmetric Bucketization 99

Quantile Bucketization 99

Feature Engineering 100

Feature Selection 106

LASSO Regression Analysis 108

Principal Component Analysis 108

Feature Importance Ranking 108

Regression Analysis 109

Decision Trees 110

Permutation Testing 111

Feature Correlation 111

Feature Imputation 113

Feature Interaction 116

Feature Visualization 118

Feature Automation 121

CHAPTER 5: MACHINE LEARNING ALGORITHMIC APPLICATION

CHAPTER 5: MACHINE LEARNING ALGORITHMIC APPLICATION 125

Machine Learning Paradigm Identification 126

Supervised Learning 127

Unsupervised Learning 129

Reinforcement Learning 131

Deep Dive: Supervised Learning Techniques & their Applications 133

Classification 133

Logistic Regression 134

Decision Trees 136

K-Nearest Neighbour (KNN) 138

Regression   140
   Linear Regression   140
   Neural Network   143
Deep Dive: Unsupervised Learning Techniques & their
Applications   145
   Clustering   146
      K-Means Clustering   146
      Gaussian Mixture Models (GMMs)   148
      Hierarchical Clustering   150
   Association   151
      Association Rule Representation   152
      Mining Association Rules   154

ACKNOWLEDGMENT   xxiii

ABOUT THE AUTHOR: JIGYASA GROVER   xxv

ABOUT THE AUTHOR: RISHABH MISRA   xxvi

LEAVE A REVIEW   xxvii

CHAPTER 1

INTRODUCTION

1 • THE MODERN BLOOM

The last couple of years have seen immense growth in the application and adoption of Machine Learning across diverse domains. There are various reasons behind this explosive growth: information overload, the need to automate mundane tasks, advancing the current state of technology, and sometimes just curiosity about the extent of possibilities.

Following are some of the applications of Machine Learning in each of the abovementioned dimensions:

• *Information Overload:* Machine Learning tackles information overload by providing recommendations based on people's liking, like suggesting what products to buy, whom to connect with, what song to listen to, and what type of content to view, all based on their past engagements and inferred interests.

- *Automation of mundane tasks:* Machine Learning automates many everyday tasks like shortlisting resumes for a job posting, identifying grammatical mistakes in a text, transcribing audio in a video or a podcast, suggesting appropriate text responses, and so on. Not having to do such mundane tasks saves much human time and effort, which could be spent on more critical tasks.

- *Advancement of technology:* Academic institutions and business corporations are also plying Machine Learning to further the present state of scientific know-how. Instances of these include developing self-driving cars, improving healthcare quality by advancing the technology to diagnose ailments in their early stages, and enhancing agriculture produce using computer vision technology to monitor crops.

- *Testing the limits:* Creative use cases of Machine Learning include creating music or meaningful lyrics without human interference, synthesizing pictures and videos of non-existent people, automatically generating food recipes, and detecting sarcasm or spoilers in a text snippet.

Unquestionably, Machine Learning is the most used and abused sub-domain of Artificial Intelligence presently. Regardless of our fascination or loathe for it, it heavily influences our decision-making power and dominates our lives presently.

To describe, enabling computers to learn on their own is what encompasses Machine Learning. The power of spotting patterns without programming is the most prominent edge these decision-making systems have over the others. Researchers keep traversing unexplored territories of Machine Learning, whereas, according to experts, the businesses have just seen the tip of the algorithmic iceberg. According to finances online, US$28.5B was allocated to Machine Learning worldwide in just the first quarter of 2019, which is staggering since the figure was only US$1.3B in 2016. Almost 50% of companies have either started exploring or are planning to incorporate Machine Learning soon. The number of startups focusing on just Machine

Learning services are having a 14x rate of increase currently. 97% of mobile users use Machine Learning trained voice assistants on their devices, with a 40% search now powered just by voice. Advancement in the software aspect has also led to the projected growth of US$120B in global sales of AI-powered hardware by the end of 2025. Enterprise domains like security, analytics, and marketing are reaching new heights with Machine Learning with a 25%, 33%, and 16% increase in adoption rates, respectively.

Dominant leaps leave the scientists, investors, policymakers, business leaders, and the audience enthralled, hinting that human-like intelligence in machines might be just around the corner. Nonetheless, progress in Machine Learning has been impressive, but there is a lot of pending explanation and examination, which keeps the research going on.

2 • SIGNIFICANCE OF DATA

For the state-of-the-art Machine Learning algorithms to work their magic, it is essential to focus on the three key dimensions:

1. Well-Calibrated Data

2. Sophisticated Algorithms

3. Efficient Computation

The algorithms mature from the iterative process of experimenting and validating hypotheses. Furthermore, efficient computation requires optimizing the algorithm using distributed processing to run on a large scale. These are absolutely the essential aspects to consider; however, laying the foundation of the process with the perfect quality and quantity of data is the secret sauce that makes Machine Learning effective.

Since we have progressed from the primeval rule-based

approach to a more data-driven approach, it goes without saying that we train Machine Learning algorithms to capture implicit patterns in the data provided. The type of data fed into the algorithm thus has a profound effect on the algorithm's success. Worthy data collection forms the foundation of the pyramid of the *AI Hierarchy of Needs* drawn parallel to *Maslow's Hierarchy of Human Needs* by Monica Rogati, a renowned Data Scientist and AI Advisor. Rogati puts forward that data literacy, data collection, and data flow form the basic needs that must be satisfied to achieve *self-actualization*, which would be the attainment of AI.

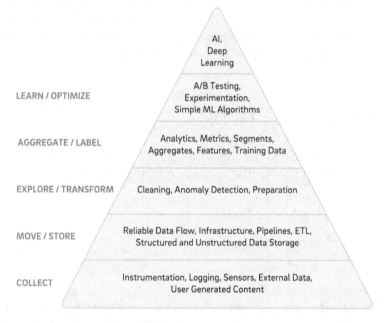

The AI Hierarchy of Needs.

With the desire to climb the Data Science ladder and contribute to the fabrication of successful Machine Learning algorithms, one should also focus on dealing with data. Before we can employ a Machine Learning solution, it is crucial to understand the problem and the data requirements, followed by researching and accumulating data from the right source.

In most cases, we cannot use the collected data *as-is*. It might need some massaging with appropriate tools and techniques. Once that is done, we can bring into play suitable learning algorithms to address the problem at hand. At this point, it is good to note and understand that no quantum of algorithmic sophistication and efficient computation can make up for the low quality and quantity of data.

Current times are witnessing accelerated advancement in intelligent systems. Just about every Machine Learning and Data Science enthusiast, conventional developer, and corporate organization is attempting to hop on the bandwagon. In that act of haste, it is widespread to skip the modus operandi of sculpting the data before training and evaluating the Machine Learning model, and eventually running into a wall. Hence, to avoid the misspending of time, money, and efforts in the race of building the perfect artificially intelligent archetype, it is pivotal to follow the process systematically.

3 • Honing Dataset Curation Skills

As we discussed above, well-calibrated data is what fuels the Machine Learning engines. There are various sources from which one can pick an already preprocessed dataset that might not require further trimming, anonymizing, standardizing, normalizing, and so on. This data can directly be fed into a model without any changes, thus providing us an easy way to get up to speed with the experimentation of sundry Machine Learning techniques. Using a preprocessed dataset also comes in handy when one just wants to check the working of the end-to-end Machine Learning pipeline; however, it might not guarantee excellent performance. There could be cases when the datasets available do not precisely match our problem's wavelength or are not present in enough quantity required by our use case. At times like these, it is convenient to synthesize our dataset and pack it up with information potentially valuable to the use case in the desired quantity. The contemporary world has volumes of all kinds of crude data available on the web. Equipped with a Machine Learning mallet, we can hammer all the nails in this data-oriented world with an added skill of identifying and extracting meaningful datasets.

I• IMPORTANCE IN ACADEMIA

World over, the scientific community engaged in higher education and research has been hustling quite a lot with Machine Learning and Data Science these days. Core Machine Learning and Data Science research groups in academia are oriented more towards novelty and advancing the field, many times weighing it higher than money-making logic or performance scaling. In this attempt to work on the new problems, finding collaborators from pertinent domains, and seeking funding for the research projects are not the only obstacles they face. They also have to look for relevant data sources in the absence of in-house data, contrary to the corporate giants who usually have access.

One way to lay hands on the relevant data is to collaborate with industry researchers; however, that is not always feasible. In that scenario, the only way to overcome this hurdle is to collect a reasonable dataset by themselves. Although challenging, many renowned academic researchers have been finding creative ways to achieve that lately. Conquering this barrier allows them to be self-sufficient and gives them a chance to lead research in new domains. Another reason curating datasets is becoming a highly regarded skill within the research community is that it fosters transparency and encourages reproducibility of the results.

II • Importance in Industry

Globally business-oriented corporations are increasingly investing in Machine Learning as they realize the value technology adds to their product and business. In contrast to academia, the industry prioritizes profit-generating logic and high scale performance higher than novelty and advancement of theoretical knowledge. Therefore, most use cases involve utilizing learning algorithms' performance on a large scale to improve the user experience or revenue generation. Established organizations seldom have obstacles in obtaining computation power, hiring folks with expertise in corresponding domains, or accessing relevant data. The challenge, however, comes in scaling up their solutions to their massive user base. Any organization would have a lot of unstructured data available on its hands as raw logs; however, developing an efficient data processing pipeline remains a task. For creating such resilient pipelines, apart from the relevant technological knowledge, we also require the skills to identify and curate meaningful and unbiased datasets from a sea of unstructured data.

4 • What Will This Book Teach?

There is a modern bloom of social networks, online shopping portals, blogs, video streaming platforms, and so many other knowledge and experience sharing platforms enabled with all kinds of media, be it textual, visual, or audio. Consequently, a vast magnitude of raw data is available via numerous sources nowadays. This book aims to provide us an in-depth guide about one of the most rudimentary aspects of Machine Learning - *Dataset Curation*.

Dataset Curation often does not get its due limelight but has high relevance in academia and industry. We shall walk through the process of constructing robust datasets from scratch using

Python[1] with tools like BeautifulSoup and Selenium. So turn the page, and start curating datasets suited to cater to all the needs!

---

1 All the scripts and high-quality version of images used in the book are available at https://gist.github.com/data-for-ml/7de6d28ab3fd0ddd487b2c3ae497e708

CHAPTER 2

DATASET EXTRACTION

THE PLANNING PHASE

Before we start this journey of *Dataset Extraction,* here is a word of caution: *Be Patient.* To build a dataset belonging to the superlative category, we would have to scout the web extensively for a start and then knead it accordingly, which is a cumbersome task. *Worry Not!* We have laid out a straightforward step-by-step process from our past experiences in academia and industry to help make the exploration systematic and efficient.

1 • Where is the Data? Overview of the Data Sources

According to David McCandless, a famous journalist and founder of the visual blog *Information Is Beautiful*, "in today's complex *information jungle*, data is the new soil". McCandless celebrates data as a ubiquitous resource providing a fertile and creative medium from which new ideas and understanding can grow.

In this modern world, all of us are inundated by information at all times. To think of data as a table filled with numbers would be an obsolete concept. There is data at more places than what we can even count. Countless things are happening every second on digital platforms: e-mails are sent and received, phrases searched in a variety of search engines, content posted on social networks, products reviewed, added to cart for online shopping, apps downloaded on different handheld and wearable devices, blogs posted, restaurants checked-in and food reviewed, stocks traded, currencies converted, and so on. The data streams are infinite, but the trick is not to let this information overwhelm; instead, hone the skills to pull out valuable insights for the social and corporate good.

2 • Sample Datasets

In simple terms, a *dataset* is a collection of related sets of information constituting separate knowledgeable elements. This book will be using a handful of datasets curated by the authors to walk through the entire data sculpting process.

Clothing Fit Dataset for Size Recommendation [1]

To improve customers' online shopping experiences and to

---

1   https://www.kaggle.com/rmisra/clothing-fit-dataset-for-size-recommendation

reduce product return rates, it is vital to have a nifty clothing size recommendation framework in place. We used *ModCloth*, an online retailer of indie and vintage-inspired women's clothing, to create datasets for this use case. This dataset contains fit feedback from customers on their purchased clothing items and other information like ratings, reviews, category information, customer measurements, etc. This dataset helps identify critical features that determine the fit of a particular clothing product size for a specific customer.

News Category Dataset [2]

We fabricated this dataset from *HuffPost*, an American news aggregator and blog. It contains around 200,000 news headlines from 2012 to 2018, having details like news category, news headlines, a short description of news stories, publication date, and so on. The dataset could be used for multiple purposes, for instance, identifying tags of untracked news articles or identifying the type of language used in different news categories.

Sarcasm Detection Dataset [3]

Past studies for sarcasm detection tasks have mostly used data from *Twitter*, a microblogging and social networking service. The data from it is collected using hashtag based supervision. However, such datasets are noisy, especially in terms of label assignments and language used. To overcome these limitations, we used *TheOnion* and *HuffPost* to create a custom dataset for our purpose. *TheOnion* is an American satirical digital media company that publishes sarcastic articles on international, national, and local news, whereas *HuffPost* reports the corresponding real news.

---

2   https://www.kaggle.com/rmisra/news-category-dataset

3   https://www.kaggle.com/rmisra/news-headlines-dataset-for-sarcasm-detection

3 • SITUATIONAL ANALYSIS

Depending on *why* we want to collect data, there are different ways to approach building good quality datasets. Considering the situation where we have a specific problem we want to address with the help of data, we have a north star, and we follow the *Guided Search* approach. If we are just curious and want some interesting data points, *Unguided Search* should be enough to fuel that wanderlust. Both these situations have their challenges, and in the following sections, we shall learn how to overcome them.

I • GUIDED SEARCH

As discussed above, when we have a specific problem in mind and have to build a dataset to address that, we go along with the *Guided Search* approach. Among the sample datasets mentioned earlier, we curated *Clothing Fit* and *Sarcasm Detection* to address specific problems, and hence these are good candidates to discuss this approach in detail.

A • CHALLENGE

The biggest challenge of the *Guided Search* of datasets is understanding the problem statement in and out. It also includes listing the essential data signals required by the Machine Learning models to address the problem completely.

B • RELEVANT DATA IDENTIFICATION

FORMAL PROBLEM DEFINTION

Before we can identify the essential data signals, we must try to define the problem formally. Let us dry run this exercise for the *Clothing Fit* and *Sarcasm Detection* datasets.

The idea behind the *Size Recommendation* problem is that we want to develop a Machine Learning model that can accurately predict a size that would fit the customer best, given product catalog sizes. So, formally we could define this problem as: *"Given past transactions of customers where they have reported the size purchased and their fit feedback, develop a Machine Learning model that takes in a future transaction and reports whether the purchase would be a fit or not."*

The idea behind *Sarcasm Detection* is that we should identify whether a particular text snippet is sarcastic or not. So we can formally define the problem as: *"Given a set of sentences where we know which ones are sarcastic and which are not, build a Machine Learning model that can take any random sentence as input and output whether it is sarcastic or not."*

ESSENTIAL DATA SIGNAL DETERMINATION

In layperson's terms, we can define a data signal as a piece of information transmitted by a particular data point. In the *Size Recommendation* problem, we want to recommend clothing sizes to customers. Based on the formal definition, we can identify the following as the essential data signals for a particular purchase: *UserID, ProductID, size purchased,* and *fit feedback*. The ID features form a vital function of tying the required information and making the data point unique. Undoubtedly, we can collect other data signals for a transaction, like *product category* or *user age*; however, they are not of absolute necessity.

The skill of identifying essential data signals comes from problem understanding and domain knowledge, and the following ways could assist in that task.

Searching the web for a legitimate source with all the required signals: This is where our *Googling* skills would come in handy. We put our web surfing expertise to use by exploring different websites and checking whether they provide all the required essential data signals or not. For example, consider *Zappos*, an online shoe and clothing retailer, for creating the *Clothing Fit* dataset. It seems promising as *Zappos* provides *UserID, ProductID, fit review*, and many other data signals. However, the missing *size purchased* signal throws a red flag. On the other hand, exploring online retailers like *ModCloth* leads us to all the above-identified essential data signals (though it might need additional tweaking; more on this later).

A typical product review page on *Zappos*.

Combining signals from multiple sources: The signal combination technique comes in handy when we cannot find a single source that provides all the essential data signals. The *Sarcasm Detection* dataset is a perfect example of combining data from multiple sources to fabricate a practical dataset. Since we know the problem (i.e., to detect the use of sarcastic tone) and the type of data we want (i.e., both sarcastic and non-sarcastic text snippets to learn the difference), we do not necessarily have to stick to one source to provide all the information. Upon a quick web search, we identified *TheOnion* as a source to get sarcastic text, and for non-sarcastic snippets, we relied on a real news reporting website like *HuffPost*.

A classic example of a sarcastic article from *TheOnion*.

DATA VOLUME REQUIREMENT

Another consideration while selecting a data source is if the source contains enough historical data to construct a sufficiently large dataset. Non-supportive instances could be when the online retailer does not have enough customer reviews reporting fit feedback, or the news source does not have an archive of old posts. The corresponding Machine Learning model might not learn suitable model parameters to capture patterns in such an underpowered dataset. In cases like these, it would be wise to combine data from multiple small sources or find a singular source to provide a large enough dataset.

At this point, there might be a question as to what is a large enough dataset. The data volume requirement is usually tied to the use case or the problem type (we shall soon discuss the different types of Machine Learning problems). For regression problems, we can come up with intervals based on the target variable range and reckon if most intervals have at least a few data points. For classification problems, we can see if the ratio of the number of data points to the number of classes is large enough. For example, 20,000 data points might be enough for 2 classes, but not for 10,000 classes.

DATA INTEGRATION FROM MULTIPLE SOURCES

This step is very open-ended and can be considered based on one's personal preference. Once we have shortlisted a data source that provides all the essential data signals and has sufficient volume, there could be different ways to further improve the dataset. An idea in that direction is to get more metadata by combining multiple sources, which might provide more data signals to our Machine Learning model. While doing that, we should always think if it would lead to better feature engineering (we shall talk more about this later) or solve a broader problem.

II• UNGUIDED SEARCH

For creative souls who are planning to fashion an exciting, distinctive yet worthwhile dataset, *Unguided Search* is what they should follow. We will refer to the *News Category* dataset to further explain the challenges and various data search problems. Since we collected the dataset without having a specific problem at hand, it is an excellent example of this approach.

A • CHALLENGE

The biggest challenge for *Unguided Search* of datasets is that it involves uncertainty to a vast extent. Since we are not sure what data signals we require in our dataset, there is no proper structure for the consequent search operation.

B • GENERAL DATA SEARCH

Although not knowing the problem makes things difficult in this case, the following dimensions try to bring some structure to our search for good quality datasets.

INTERESTING PROBLEM RECOGNITION

Does the source contain data signal(s) worth estimating?

While analyzing a website as a potential data source, we should contemplate if it provides any exciting information that is unique and worth working on with an estimation motive. It does not have to be completely out-of-the-box; it could be straightforward as the following example.

While browsing *HuffPost*, a popular American news website, we observed that each story has tags with categories (like *sports, politics, entertainment, shopping*). We thought it would be a worthy idea to predict the category given the text of the story.

Contrastingly, for a not-so-straightforward case, we collected headlines from *TheOnion* and *HuffPost* as sarcastic and non-sarcastic text snippets, respectively, and accounted for the indirect data signal of predicting whether a text snippet was sarcastic or not.

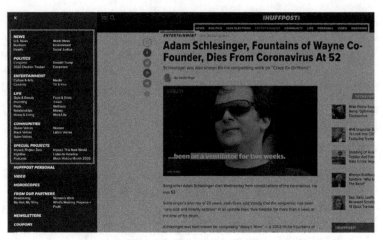

The different categories of news articles
as available on the *HuffPost*.

Does estimating the said data signal lead to fascinating results?

One of the signs of a competent dataset is that its signals can address some contemporary practical problems. Or, it could also have the ability to help us lead to fascinating insights into some phenomenon. For example, training a classifier on the *News Category* dataset could help identify any prose's writing style, whether it is *political*, has a *humorous* tone, is a *criminal* report, or is based on the latest *fashion* trends. It can also help tag untracked news articles or understand how writing styles differ for different news types.

SIDE-INFORMATION OR METADATA ASSOCIATION

According to the research publication *Patterns for Learning with Side Information* by Rico Jonschkowski, Sebastian Höfer, and Oliver Brock, *"Generalization of the learned function to unseen data can be improved by incorporating side information into learning. Side-Information are data that are neither from the input space nor from the output space of the function, but include useful information for learning it."*

Hence our dataset must have data about the data itself, which would help predict the outcome. Once a data signal is considered worth estimating, it is necessary to ensure that the web source provides enough side-information for the prediction task. If not, then we should be able to join some other data sources to make that possible. For example, predicting a product's price from just the essential data signals might not go very well if we don't have metadata around, let's say, the brand, or the fabric of the product. Thus, including a sufficient amount of side-information in the dataset helps the Machine Learning model decipher patterns better.

DATA VOLUME REQUIREMENT

The majority of the pointers in the corresponding *Guided Search* section apply here as well. Although, with a relaxed constraint that there does not exist a specific problem definition that binds us. Based on the data availability, we could modify potential problem statements. However, we have to make sure that the resulting problem is still an interesting one to solve. For example, in the *News Category* dataset, we had many categories with less than 100 headlines. Since we do not have a problem definition necessitating the prediction of infrequent classes, we can remove the corresponding records from the dataset. This way, the learning algorithm can determine better parameters for the remaining classes.

DATASET UNIQUENESS CHECK

This step is essential to ascertain that we contribute something unique and worthwhile to the community and not just repeat something that already exists on the internet.

To do a quick check, we can do simple *Google* searches for this purpose. If we find that some datasets already exist from a particular source, a refined way to contribute is to figure out the shortcomings of the prevailing datasets. It would be fruitful to ask questions like: *"Does the existing dataset come from a noisy source (i.e., are the labels not reliable)? What is the quality and quantity of side-information in the dataset? What is the size of the dataset, and can the Machine Learning model benefit from larger-scale data? Can we combine this dataset with data from a different source to create something better? How recent is the dataset?"*. It is essential to address novelty, as replicating something that already exists might not be a fair use of our time and efforts.

THE EXTRACTION PHASE

After carefully finalizing the web source, we will collect data. Let us now move on to the *Extraction Phase*, which is where the actual work gets done.

1• TOOLKIT OVERVIEW

This section will overview all the tools that we have previous experience with for curating datasets. We would be referring to these tools time and again in the book for the data extraction process. These are not necessarily the only tools for this purpose, so feel free to use any alternatives available.

I• CHROME AND CHROME DRIVER

Chrome is a widely popular cross-platform web browser developed by *Google*. Apart from being great in privacy, speed, and stability, Chrome also provides excellent tools for inspecting websites' raw code.

WebDriver is an open-source tool for automated testing of web apps across many browsers. It provides capabilities for navigating to web pages, user input, JavaScript execution, and more. *ChromeDriver* is a standalone server that implements the W3C WebDriver standard and helps automate our scraping efforts. We can download [4] a suitable version of the Chrome driver that matches our Chrome browser.

II• BEAUTIFUL SOUP

Oops, sorry to build-up the appetite; we are not talking about a delicious warm bowl of thick soup! *Beautiful Soup* is a Python library widely used to pull data out of HTML and XML files.

As we know, the browser renders each webpage from an HTML-based code. Beautiful Soup unlocks the ability to navigate quickly and modify the HTML tree structure to save us hours or days of work. Furthermore, it also allows us to write automated scripts to scrape the data from the web. To understand better, let us go over an example.

Suppose we have an HTML page coded as follows:

```
html_doc = """
    <html>
    <head><title>Humpty Dumpty</title></head>
    <body>
    <p class="title"><b>Humpty Dumpty</b></p>
    <p class="lyrics"> Humpty Dumpty sat on a
<a href="http://example.com/wall" class="noun"
```

---
4   http://chromedriver.chromium.org/downloads

```
id="link1">wall</a>, Humpty Dumpty had a great
<a href="http://example.com/fall" class="verb"
id="link2">fall</a>. All the king's <a
href="http://example.com/horses" class="horses"
id="link3">horses</a> and all the king's men,
Couldn't put Humpty together again. </p>
    <p class="lyrics">......</p>
    ......
    </body>
    </html>
"""
```

Running the above HTML document through Beautiful Soup
would give us a *BeautifulSoup* object, which represents
the document as a nested data structure as following:

```
from bs4 import BeautifulSoup
soup = BeautifulSoup(html_doc, 'lxml')
print(soup.prettify())

>>> <html>
>>>    <head>
>>>      <title>
>>>       Humpty Dumpty
>>>      </title>
>>>    </head>
>>>    <body>
>>>      <p class="title">
>>>        <b>
>>>         Humpty Dumpty
>>>        </b>
>>>      </p>
>>>      <p class="lyrics">
>>>       Humpty Dumpty sat on a
>>>        <a href="http://example.com/wall"
```

```
class="noun" id="link1">
>>>          wall
>>>          </a>
>>>      ,Humpty Dumpty had a great
>>>          <a href="http://example.com/fall"
class="verb" id="link2">
>>>          fall
>>>          </a>
>>>      . All the king's
>>>          <a href="http://example.com/horses"
class="noun" id="link3">
>>>          horses
>>>          </a>
>>>      and all the king's men, Couldn't put
Humpty together again.
>>>      </p>
>>>      <p class="lyrics">
>>>      ......
>>>      </p>
>>>      ......
>>>    </body>
>>> </html>
```

Observe the constructor, i.e., *BeautifulSoup(html_doc, 'lxml')* carefully. The *'lxml'* is an HTML parser that is lenient while parsing and runs super fast in comparison to the other kinds of parsers available. Some other parsers are:

- Python's *html.parser*: *BeautifulSoup(markup, "html.parser")*

- lxml's HTML parser: *BeautifulSoup(markup, "lxml")*

- lxml's XML parser: *BeautifulSoup(markup, "lxml-xml")* or *BeautifulSoup(markup, "xml")*

- Html5lib: *BeautifulSoup(markup, "html5lib")*

Once we have parsed and have a *BeautifulSoup* object, it is effortless to navigate the data structure, like the following.

```
soup.title
>>> <title>Humpty Dumpty</title>

soup.title.name
>>> u'title'

soup.title.string
>>> u'Humpty Dumpty'

soup.title.parent.name
>>> u'head'

soup.p
>>> <p class="title"><b>Humpty Dumpty</b></p>

soup.p['class']
>>> u'title'

soup.a
>>> <a href="http://example.com/wall"
class="noun" id="link1">wall</a>

soup.find_all('a')
>>> [ <a href="http://example.com/wall"
class="noun" id="link1">wall</a>,
<a href="http://example.com/fall" class="verb"
id="link2">fall</a>, <a href="http://example.
com/horses" class="noun" id="link3">horses</a>]

soup.find(id="link3")
```

```
>>> <a href="http://example.com/horses"
class="noun" id="link3">horses</a>
```

As we can observe from this example, it makes it easy to maneuver any given HTML document.

III• SELENIUM

Selenium is a widely used portable framework for controlling web browsers through programs. We primarily use it for automating web applications for testing purposes, and the limits of automation are endless with Selenium. It allows us to perform tasks like: launch a web browser, click on specific buttons, enter information in forms, use a search engine, etc.

Performing the day-to-day tasks using Selenium's human-like actions comes in handy when collecting data from a website, especially when the content is not static. Some websites' content may change with a click of a button or select an option from the menu. When combined with Chrome Driver, Selenium allows us to automate opening websites, navigating through the pages, mimicking button click actions, and much more.

2• BASIC RULES

Once we have narrowed down the web source to use for dataset curation and acquired the knowledge of the tools we need, it is very tempting to start scraping the content right away. Nevertheless, *Hold On!* There are always rules of a game we need to follow to ensure fair play. Hence we must follow the directives mentioned below:

1. It is crucial to read the selected web source's 'Terms &

Conditions' *before* starting the scraping process. Carefully read the statements regarding the legal use of data published on that source. Essentially, we should *not* use the data we gather from a web source for any commercial purpose.

2. Since we are using an automated tool, we need to reasonably control the number of times our tool requests data from the web source at any given time. Aggressively sweeping data could be termed as *spamming* and may break the source itself. Usually, a safe practice is to do it every second, which also mimics a human action speed.

3 • STEP-BY-STEP PROCESS

Let us use an actual example to go over this section since it would be hard to understand the process without it. We will refer to the *Clothing Fit* dataset's scraping script as an example to explain various points.

I • STRUCTURE UNDERSTANDING OF THE DATA SOURCE

The foremost thing is to navigate through the website and familiarize ourselves with the structure of the site. For a running example, let us consider the *ModCloth* website.

Exploring the website, we see that the top bar has various product categories like *dresses, tops, bottoms, swim, outerwear, shoes, accessories,* and *home*. Clicking on any one of the categories, say *tops*, we see that the products are displayed in a grid format. By default, the page shows the first 100 results, and we can see the remaining by using the scroll buttons located on the right side above the product listings.

A view of the *tops* category page on *ModCloth's* website.

Further clicking on any of the products, we know what the page looks like in the screenshot. On the product page, we have the product metadata on the top and reviews at the bottom.

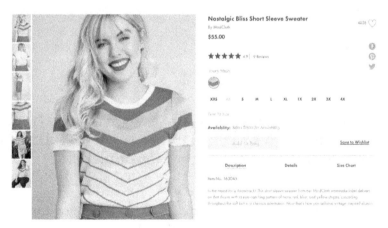

An example of the product details page on *ModCloth*.

A typical product review on *ModCloth*.

On exploring other product listings, we notice that each page contains up to 10 reviews only. If there are more than 10 reviews, the website sections them into different pages, which we can navigate using the *NEXT* button on the bottom right.

A snapshot of the *PREVIOUS* and *NEXT* navigation buttons on a product page.

One important thing to notice is that when we click the *NEXT* button, we get the next 10 reviews, but the URL does not change. This peculiarity brings us to the concept we shall be discussing in the next section about static and dynamic content. Nevertheless, to say simply, there is no other way to access the subsequent reviews apart from clicking the *NEXT* button. Similarly, a *PREVIOUS* button starts appearing to access preceding reviews. It is vital to keep track of these small yet crucial things while planning the extraction.

At this point, we would urge one to go ahead and explore the chosen web source in depth. We should note key aspects until we have a reasonably good idea of the website's structure. We should be doing this, keeping in mind the end goal of extracting reviews for each product from each of the product categories.

II • Static & Dynamic Content Extraction

Websites usually comprise two different categories of content: *static* and *dynamic*. The fixed content of a website is called the *static* part. It displays the same content for every user regardless of anything else and is usually written purely in HTML. On the other hand, the *dynamic* part is curated on the fly. In our case, it depends on which user has logged in and their interactions, making use of advanced programming scripts like PHP, ASP, JSP, and so on. How to render dynamic content is beyond this book's scope; however, knowing it exists is essential for us to streamline our scraping efforts.

Considering the above, one can imagine that extracting content from a static webpage is more straightforward than a dynamic webpage. With a fixed URL pointing to a static page that remains unaffected by any user actions, simple tools like *Python Request Library* can extract the content. For example, following we show passing a URL of a static page to the requests object will return HTML page contents in the form of *<Element html at 0x211954a0c28>*. We can scrape this content easily using *BeautifulSoup* as demonstrated in one of the previous sections:

```
import requests
from lxml import html

html_page = requests.get( 'https://
```

```
en.wikipedia.org/wiki/Static_web_page' )
print (html_page)
>>> <Response [200]>

html_code = tree = html.fromstring(html_page.
content)
print (html_code)
>>> <Element html at 0x211954a0c28>
```

Nonetheless, we can not use the same process for extracting dynamic content. The contents displayed are not tied to a URL, and they keep changing with the user actions. That is where *Selenium* comes in handy, as it can mimic user actions like a click of a button, filling of the form, etc., and also return the corresponding HTML page. Since most websites rely on server-side and client-side scripts these days, it is vital to learn how to scrape the content and automate it. In the following section, we will learn how to extract such dynamic content.

III• KEY INFORMATION ACQUISITION

Keeping in mind the goal of extracting reviews for each product from each of the *ModCloth* product categories, we identify the critical pieces of information as *product details* and *reviews*. Let us go through each of these separately to understand better.

A• PRODUCT LINKS' EXTRACTION

As we saw previously, there are a fixed number of categories for products on *ModCloth* like *dresses, tops, bottoms, swim, outerwear, shoes, accessories, wedding,* and *home*. Hence, it is not necessary to write a script to extract their links. Surprisingly, manually doing this would be more efficient and faster. The links would be something as following:

- Dress category: https://www.modcloth.com/shop/dresses

- Shoes category: https://www.modcloth.com/shop/shoes

- Accessories category: https://www.modcloth.com/shop/accessories

This section focuses on extracting links of different products from one of these categories, say *tops*. We examined that within each category, the website presents products in groups of 102 on each page. We can view the next 102 using the scroll buttons located on the top right above the product listings. For each of the 102 products, we have a page scroller to access all of them vertically.

First, we notice how the links for various pages vary, and it follows a pattern:

- Page 1: https://www.modcloth.com/shop/tops?&sz=102&start=0

- Page 2: https://www.modcloth.com/shop/tops?&sz=102&start=102

- Page 3: https://www.modcloth.com/shop/tops?&sz=102&start=204

For each page, we now need to extract the links to each of the products. Let us make use of the *inspect* functionality of a web browser. This functionality would let us see behind the scenes of that particular element, including the source code, images, CSS, fonts and icons, Javascript code that powers animations, and much more.

Using Google Chrome to inspect the
link to a product on *ModCloth*.

To use this feature, right-click on the element and go to the
`inspect` option. Next, identify the anchor element, i.e.,
`<a>`, that contains the product's link and note its CSS class
specifically. In the following example, we see that the CSS
class is `thumb-link`. Usually, all the product links would
be using the same class, but it is better to verify it.

Using the information we have gathered above, we can
write the following code to extract all the products' links
in the *tops* category.

```
import time
from bs4 import BeautifulSoup
from selenium import webdriver

# download driver from chromedriver.chromium.
org/downloads
path_to_chromedriver = './chromedriver.exe'
browser = webdriver.Chrome(executable_path =
path_to_chromedriver)

urls = []
counter = 0
tops_link = []
```

```
# since the tops category has 7 pages, where
link to each follows a specific pattern
identified above, we can create links to them as
following:

for i in range(7):
  urls.append( 'https://www.modcloth.com/shop/
tops?sz=102&start=' + str(counter))
  counter += 102

# extracting links for products in each page
for url in urls:
  # open the url
  browser.get(url)
  # purposeful wait time to allow the website
to get fully loaded
  time.sleep(4)
  # get page content
  content = browser.page_source

  soup = BeautifulSoup(content, "lxml")

  product_links = []
  # extract all the anchor i.e., <a> elements
with "thumb-link" class from the page
  data_links = soup.find_all("a",
{"class":"thumb-link"})

  # from each <a> element, extract the URL
  for i in data_links:
    product_links.append('https://www.modcloth.
com' + i['href'])

  tops_link.extend(product_links)
  # purposeful wait time to avoid sending
requests in quick succession
```

```
time.sleep(10)
```

Note the purposeful wait times included in the script above. We do this to ensure the website loads properly before extracting the content and wait before sending another request to avoid overloading. Recalling the basic rules we discussed before, it is good to have a single request per second to mirror human behavior. However, given that *ModCloth* is a relatively smaller website (if we compare the scale to *Amazon*), we might want to have a longer wait time. One is free to use their judgment in this aspect, but we should just be mindful.

B• PRODUCT REVIEWS' EXTRACTION

Now that we have a link for each product in the *tops* categories, we can go deeper and extract reviews for each of them. Let us inspect what the HTML code looks like for each review entity.

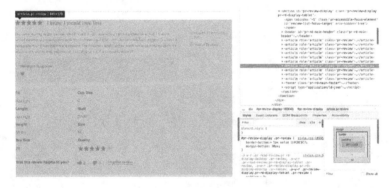

Inspecting a customer review.

We notice that each review is contained in an `<article>` element with a class named `pr-review`. Let us explore inside one of the `<article>` elements by clicking the small arrow button towards the left side to unnest.

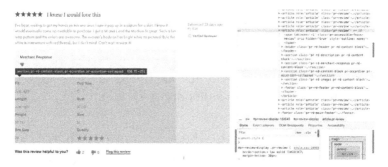

Inspecting the structured component of a customer review.

As we hover on various components inside the `<article>` tag, the corresponding view gets highlighted on the webpage. Seeing in the image above, there is a `<section>` element with a CSS class named *pr-rd-content-block pr-accordion pr-accordion-collapsed*. It corresponds to the feedback regarding the fit of the product and also the measurements of the customer. Similarly, other parts of the review are present under different `<section>` elements. Digging deep into the `<section>` element, we notice that they are further nested inside a `<div>` element with a class named *pr-accordion-content*.

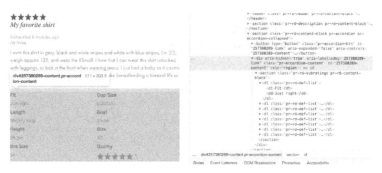

Inspecting the fit feedback component of a customer review.

We have a *definition list* inside of it, i.e., `<dl>` element with the class name `pr-rd-def-list`, where each element corresponds to a fit feedback signal or a customer measurement. The `<dt>` element contains the raw text for the field name and `<dd>` tag contains the field value. The key-value structure might remind us of the dictionary data structure in Python. Our final goal is to extract these feedback signals in a dictionary format.

Armed with the above knowledge, we are now extracting the fit feedback signals from the reviews of *tops* category products:

Setting up an automated browser using Selenium.

```
from bs4 import BeautifulSoup
from selenium import webdriver

# download driver from http://chromedriver.
chromium.org/downloads
path_to_chromedriver = './chromedriver.exe'
browser = webdriver.Chrome(executable_path =
path_to_chromedriver)
```

For each product page in the *tops* category, extracting the review content on the landing page.

```
scraped_data = []

for i in range(0,len(tops_link)):
    url = tops_link[i]

    # open a product's landing page
    browser.get(url)
```

```
# get the webpage content
content = browser.page_source
soup = BeautifulSoup(content, "lxml")
```

Extracting all the reviews' raw content.

```
review_data = soup.find_all("article", {"class":
"pr-review"})
```

For each review, we extract fit feedback and customer measurements.

```
review_metadata_raw = []
for i in range(len(review_data)):
    review_metadata_raw.append(review_data[i].
find("div", {"class": "pr-accordion-content"}))
```

From the raw review data we make a list of lists.

```
review_metadata_elements = [review_metadata_
raw[i].find_all("dl", {"class", "pr-rd-def-
list"}) for i in range(len(review_metadata_
raw))]
```

Finally, extracting details in a dictionary format.

```
review_metadata = []
for element in review_metadata_elements:
    # <dt> elements contain metadata field names
like "fit", "length", etc.
    # <dd> elements contain reviewer's response
```

```
for those metadata fields like "small", "just
right", etc.
  review_metadata.append(
    {
      element[i].find("dt").text.lower(),
      element[i].find("dd").text.lower()
    } for i in range(len(element))
  )
scraped_data.extend(review_metadata)
```

IV• Process Automation

In the previous section, we successfully wrote a script to
extract reviews from each product's landing page in the
website's *tops* category. *Yayy!* However, we still are far from
our final goal of creating a dataset from the entire website.
This section would help us repeat the same task for each
product category without much human assistance.

To automate the script, we have to figure out how to
automatically navigate to other review pages by clicking the
NEXT button or mimicking that action using Selenium.

A snapshot of the *NEXT* navigation button
on a product page.

```
browser.execute_script(
  "arguments[0].click();",
  browser.find_element_by_xpath(<BUTTON_XPATH>)
)
```

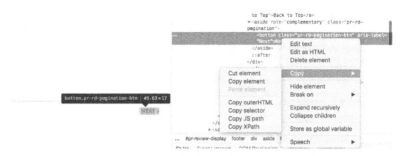

The approach to finding the *XPath* for the
NEXT button on Google Chrome.

Grasping   the above snippet might also require an
understanding of what exactly *XPath* is. To make it easier,
think of *XPath* as a way to navigate through the elements
and attributes in an HTML document. It is like a unique
address for each HTML document component, which in the
above example is present in the *BUTTON_XPATH* placeholder.
To identify the *XPath* of an element, we again use the inspect
feature, as shown above.

For example, filling the required *NEXT* button's *XPath* in
the example snippet would lead us to something like the
following:

```
browser.execute_script(
  "arguments[0].click();",
  browser.find_element_by_xpath(
    '//*[@id="pr-review-display"]/footer/div/
aside/button'
  )
)
```

Paying close attention to the website's structure, we notice
that once we click the *NEXT* button to go to reviews beyond
the first page, a *PREVIOUS* button pops up, which was

41

missing on the landing review page. *Yes!* It is correct to think that the introduction of the *PREVIOUS* button changes the *XPath* of the *NEXT* button.

A snapshot of the *PREVIOUS* and *NEXT*
navigation buttons on a product page.

Inspecting the elements all over again and extracting the respective *XPath*, we find that they change from the second page onwards, leading to the following Selenium script changes.

```
browser.execute_script(
   "arguments[0].click();",
   browser.find_element_by_xpath(
      '//*[@id="pr-review-display"]/footer/div/
aside/button[2]'
   )
)
```

Combining all the above findings, let us update the script we made previously to automate the process.

Iterate over all review pages of the product before content extraction.

```
# Repeat until we run out of review pages
while(True):
   # Get the webpage content
   content = browser.page_source
```

```
soup = BeautifulSoup(content, "lxml")
......
......
```

**Mimic the click of *NEXT* button after appending *review_
metadata* to *scraped_data* to jump to the next page (if
available) else break the infinite loop introduced above.**

```
......
scraped_data.extend(review_metadata)

# If current page is the initial one, it
contains only NEXT button
if init == 0:
  try:
    init = 1
    # Execute click on NEXT by utilizing the
XPath of NEXT
    browser.execute_script(
      "arguments[0].click();",
      browser.find_element_by_xpath(
        '//*[@id="pr-review-display"]/footer/
div/aside/button'
      )
    )
  except NoSuchElementException:
    # No NEXT button present, less than 10
reviews
    break
else:
  try:
    browser.execute_script(
      "arguments[0].click();",
      browser.find_element_by_xpath(
        '//*[@id="pr-review-display"]/footer/
```

```
div/aside/button[2]'
      )
   )
 except NoSuchElementException:
   # No NEXT button, no more pages left
   break
```

NoSuchElementException is widely used to throw an exception when the selector used to find an element does not return a *WebElement*. We can import this Selenium exception as:

```
from selenium.common.exceptions import
NoSuchElementException
```

By this step, our script is entirely ready to extract all the reviews across multiple pages from the products in the *tops* categories. This step would be the end if we were in a perfect world. *Alas!* While running this script in its current form, we might get some errors that might disrupt our data collection process. The next section will help us handle the errors gracefully.

V • ERROR HANDLING

We need to learn to identify the failure points, especially if we want our script to run smoothly. However, like most times in life, *we do not know what we do not know!* To start the process of error handling, we will first be doing a *dry run* of our script. We will identify points where we have the potential of a mishap and update the script accordingly. Following, we describe some instances that came across while we were doing a trial run at our end and how we handled them.

1. While trying to fetch the product details from a web page, we found that the URL was invalid. Some potential reasons for this could be that the website is not well maintained or recently updated. Hence, the old and new URLs were not compatible anymore. We handled this by using a *WebDriverException* in Selenium, which throws an error if the required session does not exist or is invalid in format.

```
from selenium.common.exceptions import
WebDriverException
. . . . . .
. . . . . .
# Open the URL in browser
try:
    browser.get(url)
except WebDriverException:
    # If the extracted URL is invalid
    print('invalid url', iterr)
    continue
. . . . . .
. . . . . .
```

2. At times, the review metadata was not present when we were trying to extract it. This absence led to the entire script's failure, and we combated it by placing validity checks at various places before pulling the data.

```
review_metadata_elements = [
    review_metadata_raw[i].find_all(
        "dl", {"class", "pr-rd-def-list"}
    )
    if review_metadata_raw[i] is not None
    else None
```

```
  for i in range(len(review_metadata_raw))
]

review_metadata = []

for element in review_metadata_elements:
  if element is None:
    review_metadata.append(None)
    continue
  review_metadata.append([(
      element[i].find("dt").text.lower(),
      element[i].find("dd").text.lower()
    ) for i in range(len(element))
  ])
```

3. There were times when the content extracted was *null* despite the corresponding page having all the information. It was mostly happening because the website took some time to load all the contents, and by that time, the extraction code would have already run. We introduced a sleep time to let the web page load before we started the extraction process.

```
browser.get(url)
time.sleep(4)
content = browser.page_source
soup = BeautifulSoup(content, "lxml")
```

4. When we thought our script was fool-proof, we tried running it end-to-end for different cases. Even then, we came across some issues that thwarted our progress: we got disconnected from the internet, or our laptops ran out of battery. Several other scenarios can also lead to a loss of progress. Keeping track of which iteration the process was interrupted will help us resume from the same point rather than starting all over again. For example, you can

save the *NumPy* array like following:

```
np.save('./scraped_data_tops.npy',scraped_
data)
```

VI• Request Rate Limitations

In simpler terms, the *request rate* for a website is the number of times per unit time it can handle returning a valid response without getting overloaded. It is of utmost importance that we respect the rate-limiting scale of a website by reasonably controlling the number of requests we make. Our uncontrolled behavior could bring down a website. Moreover, many websites have a *fail-safe* design feature that automatically blocks an IP, which sends unusually high traffic.

To avoid getting blocked or disrupt regular website traffic, we must have an unavoidable lag between two web page load requests. For instance, whenever we mimic the *NEXT* button's clicking to access the review pages, we are making a load request. Hence we need to introduce a wait time between the two points of action, which we can do in the following manner.

```
# If the current page is the initial one, it
contains only NEXT button (PREVIOUS is missing)
if init == 0:
  try:
    init = 1
    browser.execute_script(
      "arguments[0].click();",
      browser.find_element_by_xpath(
        '//*[@id="pr-review-display"]/footer/
```

```
div/aside/button'
        )
    )
    time.sleep(10 + random.randint(0,5))
  except NoSuchElementException:
    # No NEXT button present, that is less than
10 reviews
    time.sleep(15 + random.randint(0,10))
    break
else:
  try:
    # Execute click on NEXT by utilizing the
XPath of NEXT
    # XPath of NEXT is different here since
PREVIOUS is also present
    browser.execute_script(
      "arguments[0].click();",
      browser.find_element_by_xpath(
        '//*[@id="pr-review-display"]/footer/
div/aside/button[2]'
      )
    )
    time.sleep(10 + random.randint(0,5))
  except NoSuchElementException:
    # No NEXT button present, that is less than
10 reviews
    time.sleep(15 + random.randint(0,10))
    break
```

We went a step further and introduced an element of randomness in our wait times to conceal the certainty that the incoming requests are automated. It is up to us to choose how much wait time we would want between each load request based on the website in question, data requirement, time constraints, and resources available. However, it should always be sufficient enough to overcome the rate-limiting factor.

4 • EXPECTED OUTCOME

After the script's successful execution, the content collected from the website would be present in the variable *scraped_ data* in the form of a dictionary containing the product details, customer measurements, and the review text. Here is a sneak-peek into what the result should looklike:

```
. . . . . .
{
    'bra size': '42',
    'category': 'tops',
    'cup size': 'd',
    'fit': 'slightly small',
    'height': '5ft 6in',
    'hips': '46.0',
    'product_id': '149377',
    'length': 'just right',
    'original_size': 'xxxl',
    'product_sizes': {'l', 'm', 's', 'xl', 'xs',
'xxl', 'xxxl'},
    'quality': '4rated 4 out of 5 stars',
    'review_summary': 'I love love love this shi',
    'review_text': "I love love love this shirt. I
ordered up because it looked a little more fitted in
the picture, and I'm glad I did; if I had ordered
my normal size it would probably have been snugger
than I prefer. The material is good qualityit's
semithick. And the design is just so hilariously
cute! I'm going to see if this brand has other tees
and order more.",
```

```
  'shoe size': '8.00',
  'shoe width': 'average',
  'size': 16,
  'user_name': 'erinmbundren'
}
......
```

CHAPTER 3

DATASET PREPARATION

After completing the data extraction phase in the previous chapter, we now have the desired data in a structured format. It marks a significant milestone in our journey of creating a meaningful dataset, but there is more to it before we reach our end goal. We have to work on the extracted data to eliminate impurities that might have crept in before feeding into a Machine Learning model. There are several facets of the *Data Preparation* phase that we shall explore in this chapter.

1• DATA TRIMMING

Recall our discussion regarding essential *data signals* when we had to identify relevant data sources. As mentioned previously, our data would not help a Machine Learning model, no matter how sophisticated the model is, if the essential data signals are missing. Regarding the online retailer *ModCloth*, the website allows its customers to give detailed fit feedback, which is critical to address the *Size Recommendation* problem. However, we notice that not all customer reviews mention the fit (like the example below).

A few examples of reviews missing the critical
fit feedback component on *ModCloth*.

It is evident that the data we collected might have a certain percentage of reviews with no fit feedback. These reviews are of no use to us since they are missing the essential data signals. Therefore, we need to either remove these transactions from our data or find a way to produce the essential data signals with the information we have.

In technical terms, this process of excluding specific values due to their irrelevance, redundancy, or extremity from a dataset is known as *Data Trimming*. Believing that more training data yields a better generalization of the Machine Learning algorithm is one of the many misconceptions in this domain. The quality of training examples matters to quite an extent. It has been experimentally proven that a model performs better when discarding some, especially noisy, training examples. Data Trimming is synonymous with *Data Pruning*, in many other materials available on this subject.

Let us review some specific scenarios with respect to the raw data scraped from *ModCloth* previously:

1. Many reviews do not contain fit feedback or provide any information regarding the product sizing, as discussed above. These do not align well for the purpose of our *Size Recommendation* problem.

A few examples of reviews missing the critical
fit feedback component on *ModCloth*.

2. If we recall, we had collected each review in the form of a dictionary. The dictionary also had *fit* and *size* as the keys, indicating the feedback regarding the product's fit and the size of the product purchased, respectively. Since these are essential data signals, we can eliminate the records that have missing values for these keys, as follows:

```
trimmed_data = []
for record in scraped_data:
    if 'fit' in record.keys() and 'size' in record.
keys():
        trimmed_data.append(record)
```

3. Information about the customer/user who purchased a product and left a review on the website is also valuable. *ModCloth* assigns each product a unique identifier; however, it does not have a unique ID for the reviewers. Instead, the website only mentions the name of each reviewer, which has a high chance of not being unique. The absence of distinctive identifiers is challenging since we identified *UserID* as an

essential data signal for the *Size Recommendation* problem along with *ProductID, size purchased,* and *fit feedback.*

The reviews on *ModCloth* do not seem to be associated with unique *UserIDs*.

Many reviews on the website include vital details regarding a user, like body measurements, which are highly correlated to the size purchased and the consequential fit feedback. Since the user's body measurements are identifiable details and unique to a great degree, we can use those in conjunction with the reviewer name to build individual identities.

To create a unique identifier and ensure that no two users get assigned the same one (which is quite possible with the names), we consider the body measurement attributes. We use three or more body measurements from the set of eight different ones, viz. *height, bust, bra size, cup size, hips, waist, shoe size,* and *shoe width,* to create a unique identifier by combining them with the user name. This process ensures that users who have provided at least three body measurements get assigned an identifier. Consequently, we can remove the records from the dataset that are not associated with an identifier.

```
trimmed_data = []
unique_users = set()
user_measurement_attributes = {
    'height',
    'bra size',
    'cup size',
    'bust',
    'hips',
    'waist',
    'shoe size',
    'shoe width'
}

for record in scraped_data:
    attributes_present = len(set(record.keys())&
user_measurement_attributes)
    if attributes_present < 3:
        # Since the user can not be uniquely
identified,
        # we skip that review/record
        continue
    unique_user_name = record['user_name'].lower()
    unique_user_name = unique_user_name
        + (record['height'] if 'height' in record
else '')
        + (record['bra size'] if 'bra size' in
record else '')
        + (record['cup size'] if 'cup size' in
record else '')
        + (record['bust'] if 'bust' in record else
'')
        + (record['hips'] if 'hips' in record else
'')
        + (record['waist'] if 'waist' in record else
'')
        + (record['shoe size'] if 'shoe size' in
```

```
record else '')
    + (record['shoe width'] if 'shoe width' in
record else '')
  record['unique_user_name'] = unique_user_name

  if unique_user_name not in unique_users:
    unique_users.add(unique_user_name)

  trimmed_data.append(record)
```

A point to be noted is that here we assign each user an identifier, which is a combination of the user's name and their body measurements. In the upcoming section of *Data Anonymization*, we shall be discussing how we will use this to assign a unique *UserID* to each.

4. On further data analysis, we find some reviews where the customer's reported size was not present in the catalog of sizes for the corresponding product. The missing sizes could be due to reporting errors, thus resulting in data discrepancies. It is crucial to remove them from the set of records so that the model does not end up training on that particular piece of misinformation. To sanitize this, first, we need to collect all the sizes available for a specific product and cross-check if the reported size of the product purchased in the review belongs to the set or not.

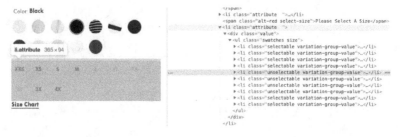

Inspecting the available catalog sizes for a particular product.

For instance, to do this for products in the *tops* category, we first *inspect* the sizes section on *ModCloth*'s product page. We see that they are present inside an unordered HTML list (`<ul>`) attribute with the class name `swatches size`. Using this piece of information, we do something like below:

```
product_sizes = {}
for iterr in range(len(top_links)):
  init = 0
  flag = 0
  count = 0
  url = tops_links[iterr]

  try:
    browser.get(url)
    time.sleep(4)
  except WebDriverException:
    print('invalid url', iterr)
    continue

  content = browser.page_source
  soup = BeautifulSoup(content, "lxml")
  product_id = soup.find("div", {"class":
"product-number"}).find("span").text

  try:
    product_sizes[product_id] = [i.text.strip()
for i in soup.find("ul", {"class": "swatches
size"}).find_all("li")]
  except AttributeError:
    print('sizes not available for ', product_
id)

  time.sleep(10 + random.randint(0,10))
```

Then we can prune the data records simply like the following:

```
trimmed_data = []
for record in scraped_data:
  if record['size'] in product_
sizes[record[product_id]]:
    trimmed_data.append(record)
```

The above discussion and examples help us understand how noisy data could be detrimental to a learning algorithm and how we can use simple techniques to remove sub-optimal records from a dataset. This data trimming stage significantly reduces the dataset's size and gives us a clean version of the data. Using this clean data in training the model, we might boost its generalization capability.

2 • DATA ANONYMIZATION

Nowadays, government agencies around the world are strictly enforcing user privacy and data protection laws. For giant multinational corporations, user data is like a gold mine. In the absence of appropriate checks, the corporations can easily use and abuse it to their advantage. Acknowledging this sensitive issue, it is our responsibility to satisfy the data privacy requirements while building a dataset so that it is safe to release it publicly.

The process of safeguarding private and sensitive information by deleting or encrypting personally identifiable information from a dataset is called *Data Anonymization*. Full name, social security number, driver's license number, bank account number, passport number, and email address are some examples of *Personally Identifiable Information (PII)* that someone can use to identify a particular person. Data Anonymization enables safe data usage for various purposes with a reduced risk of unintentional disclosure of sensitive data.

There are multiple techniques for anonymization of the data, some of them are as follows:

1. Masking: This technique involves concealing data with altered values. A simple example could be character substitution, like replacing *"X"* with *"*"*, *"4"* with *"&"*, *"H"* with *"#"*, and so on. It is necessary to map the symbols without a particular pattern to avoid de-anonymization risk.

2. Pseudonymization: This method demands substituting specific identifiers with fakely fabricated identifiers, thus preserving statistical accuracy and maintaining data integrity. For instance, one could replace the full name *"Raquel Murillo"* with *"Lisbon"* (*Money Heist* fans would understand this better!)

3. Generalization: In this approach, we deliberately discard some information from our set to make it less identifiable while still maintaining data accuracy. A simple example could be that we remove the house numbers in a set of user addresses but retain the street names.

4. Shuffling: This is a very widely used method where we shuffle one of the data columns containing PII so that the new value and the attributes of the remaining record do not help in unique identification.

5. Perturbation: This technique involves altering the numbers by rounding them off using a base number and adding noise. Using small numbers as a base leads to weak anonymization, whereas large numbers might disrupt data accuracy. Hence the range of values needs to be in proportion to the perturbation. For example, we can round off users' age using a base of 4 because we still retain the proportionality, whereas using 14 would seem fake at first glance itself.

6. Synthesis: In this method, we fabricate synthetic data with no connection to the real situation using patterns found in the dataset. This process leads to artificially creating the data and replacing PII for protecting data.

In our case, the data scraped from *ModCloth* contains sensitive information for a user, which includes the body measurements like *height, bust, bra size, cup size, hips, waist, shoe size,* and *shoe width*. Following the acceptable practices of building a quality dataset, we must remove any information from the dataset that could assist an ill-intentioned person in tracing the exact review for a product by that user and exploiting them. We can achieve this by applying the *synthesis* technique discussed above to artificially generate synthetic data of random numbers and replace the original *UserID* and *ProductID*. Further, we can remove the links to the product and mask product names to minimize the risk of tracing back to the exact review. This practice is all the more essential if we extracted the data from a source that is not public and requires proper authentication for data access, i.e., logging-in before accessing the website and reading reviews.

```
import numpy as np

user_index = {}
product_index = {}
base_user = np.random.randint(0,10000)
base_product = np.random.randint(0,10000)

for record in trimmed_data:
    if record['unique_user_name'] not in user_index:
        user_index[record['unique_user_name']] = base_
user + np.random.randint(0,200)
        base_user += 200
```

```
record['user_id'] = str(user_
index[record['unique_user_name']])

if record['product_id'] not in product_index:
    product_index[record['product_id']] = base_
product + np.random.randint(0,200)
    base_product += 200

record['product_id'] = product_
index[record['product_id']]
```

3 • DATA STANDARDIZATION

One of the critical traits of a good quality dataset is interpretability; different people should comprehend the dataset precisely as we intended it to be. Since we collect data with more than a handful of attributes, it is highly probable that those values are in different notations across different records.

A simple case could be the *date of birth* field, with some values in the *MM-DD-YYYY* format and some in *DD/MM/YYYY* format. Another example could be the *state* field where some mention the entire string like *CALIFORNIA,* while others cite the two-letter code like *CA*. While these examples might seem trivial at first, elements like these could limit the learning capability of a Machine Learning model; the same date in different formats would be considered two different objects, which impacts model parameter tuning.

The process of enforcing standards on data so that the attributes are in the same format is called *Data Standardization.* We can achieve this via domain knowledge, intuition, or experimentation. Adopting a standard may require a significant investment of time and skill, but *better input yields better output;* Machine Learning models trained on standardized inputs may be able to generalize and perform better.

In our example, we observe that there are cases where products have different sizing conventions. For instance, some products in the *bottoms* category are sized on the US scale, while others on the UK scale. We also see such differences in other clothing categories. It is important to note that our *Size Recommendation* problem is of the *ordinal regression* type. That is, we have to predict an ordinal variable (a.k.a. size) whose value exists on an arbitrary scale, and only the relative ordering between different values is essential. Therefore we must establish an order between all the different sizes available from the data source; otherwise, we cannot use the data for the problem at hand. Establishing order is not a challenging task if all the products follow the same sizing convention, but it becomes harder for products sized on different scales.

An example showcasing different sizing conventions for different products on *ModCloth*.

• One way to handle this challenge is by utilizing the sizing chart available on *ModCloth*. The sizing chart maps sizes from different conventions to help create a standard scale that preserves the order. However, we came across some scenarios where certain products' sizes were not present in the chart. For instance, the *XXXS* size is not present on the size chart. In that case, we can either convert it to our standard scale by using the knowledge that it would be smaller than *XXS* (which is present in the size chart) or discard the record entirely.

• However, using the size mapping chart does not solve all our problems. For instance, several *bottoms* category products might have the same size but have different *length, hips,* or *waist* measurements. We can see that sizes *24, 26, 28,* and *30* have two different measurements. The bottom left chart is from a *jeans* family whereas the chart on the right is from a *dress* one.

Size Chart

Size	Bust	Waist	Hips
XXS	30	22	32
XS	31-32	23-24	33-34
S	33-34	25-26	35-36
M	35-36	27-28	37-38
L	37-39	29-31	39-41
XL	40-43	32-35	42-45
XXL	45-47	37-39	47-49
1X	43-45	35-37	45-47
2X	46-48	38-40	48-50
3X	50-53	42-45	52-55

Size Chart

US ∨	Bust	Waist	Hips
00	31	23	33
0	32	24	34
2	33	25	35
4	34	26	36
6	35	27	37
8	36	28	38
10	37 $\frac{1}{2}$	29 $\frac{1}{2}$	39 $\frac{1}{2}$
12	39	31	41
14	41	33	43
16	43	35	45
18	45	37	47
20	46 $\frac{1}{2}$	38 $\frac{1}{2}$	48 $\frac{1}{2}$
22	48	40	50
24	50 $\frac{1}{2}$	42 $\frac{1}{2}$	52 $\frac{1}{2}$
26	53	45	55
28	55	47	57 $\frac{1}{2}$
30	57	49	60

Size Chart

US ∨	Waist	Hip
24	24	35
25	25	36
26	26	37
27	27	38
28	28	39
29	29	40
30	30	41
31	31	42
32	32	43

The different size charts available on *ModCloth*.

To handle conflicting sizes when they occur in a review, we can look at all the catalog sizes available for the corresponding product. If the smallest size does not appear in the *jeans'* size mapping, we can use the *dress* one. Hence, based on our observation of measurements corresponding to different sizes, we can develop a map representing the ordering of sizes across other conventions.

```
size_map_bottom = {'0':1, '1':2, '2':3, '3':4,
'4':5, '5':6, '6':7, '7':8, '8':9, '9':10,
'10':11, '11':12, '12':13, '13':14, '14':15,
'14w':16, '15':17, '16':18, '16w':19, '18':21,
'18w':22, '20':24, '20w':25, '22':27, '22w':28,
```

```
'24':30, '24w':31, '26':33, '26w':34, '28':36,
'28w':37, '30':39, '30w':40, '6uk':3, '8uk':5,
'10uk':7, '12uk':9, '14uk':11, '16uk':13,
'18uk':15, '20uk':18, '22uk':21, '24uk':24,
'26uk':27, '28uk':30, '30uk':33, 'xxs':0,
'xs':1, 's':4, 'sm':6, 'm':8, 'ml':10, 'l':12,
'lxl':14, 'xl':15, '1x':20, '1x2x':23, '2x':26,
'3x':32, '3x4x':35, '4x':38, 'xxl':23,
'xxxl':31}

size_map_jeans = {'24':1, '25':2, '26':4,
'27':5, '28':8, '29':9, '30':12, '31':13}

conflicting_sizes = {'24', '26', '28', '30'}
```

Once we have the above mappings, we can use the following snippet to standardize our data:

```
for record in trimmed_data:
  if record['category'] == 'bottoms':
    if record['size'] in conflicting_sizes:
      if product_sizes[record['product_id']][0]
== '24':
        record['size'] = size_map_
jeans[record['size']]
      else:
        record['size'] = size_map_
bottom[record['size']]
    elif record['size'] in size_map_bottom:
      record['size'] = size_map_
bottom[record['size']]
    else:
      record['size'] = size_map_
jeans[record['size']]
```

The above-discussed example is when we can perform standardization of the data via a simple mapping technique. In reality, when we build datasets for several complex purposes, multiple attributes require the alignment of data definitions, representation, and structure. Hence, keep in mind that Data Standardization is a core methodology to facilitate the connectivity, consistency, and synchronization of information and nurture data's quality.

4 • Data Integration

In an ideal scenario, we can build a dataset using a single web source only, like from *ModCloth*. However, there would be circumstances when we would have to gather bits of attributes from multiple sources to have a more inclusive, meaningful, and valuable dataset. Coalescing the data from separate sources to provide a unified view is known as *Data Integration*. The outcome of this stage is a seamlessly fused set of data records that we could then feed into a Machine Learning model. From a broader point of view, there are two types of Data Integration processes:

I • Vertical Integration

Recall the dataset we referred to for the *Sarcasm Detection* problem, where we collected the data from two different websites: *TheOnion* and *HuffPost*. *TheOnion* provided sarcastic versions of current affairs, whereas *HuffPost* reported real and non-sarcastic news. To create a final dataset, we fused the records collected from the respective sources by appending them *vertically*. Since the attributes in both the sets were similar, namely *article link, headline*, and `is_sarcastic` *label*, it was easier to connect them to form a dataset having both sarcastic and non-sarcastic records.

While we are in the Data Integration stage, we need to be mindful of deliberately breaking the observed patterns in the respective datasets and, consequently, in the combined one. For example, while we are processing the data from *TheOnion* and *HuffPost* sequentially to integrate them, it is evident that the final dataset would have all the sarcastic records first followed by the non-sarcastic news records.

Let us assume that we do not break this pattern and feed it into a standard predictive model. The models typically require an $80:20$ split for the training dataset and evaluation dataset. We would be in trouble since the training dataset would be imbalanced, having more sarcastic news records than non-sarcastic records. Moreover, the evaluation dataset would have all of the non-sarcastic news! Hence, to overcome this issue, we break the pattern by shuffling the dataset after appending the records from two sources to curate a balanced dataset, something as follows:

```python
import random

data = []

for record in sarcastic_data:
    temp = dict()
    temp['is_sarcastic'] = 1
    temp['headline'] = record['headline']
    temp['article_link'] = record['link']
    data.append(temp)

for record in non_sarcastic_data:
    temp = dict()
    temp['is_sarcastic'] = 0
    temp['headline'] = record['headline']
    temp['article_link'] = record['link']
    data.append(temp)
```

```
random.shuffle(data)
```

II • Horizontal Integration

Let us consider a task where we have to build a dataset regarding different cities globally containing specific fields: *state, country, area, population, climate, pollution, civic administration, religion, languages, festivals,* and *cuisine*. It is highly probable that we would need to refer to multiple sources from the web to gather all the information. Some attributes like *state, country, area,* and *population* might be available from one source, whereas information about *demographics* and *culture* from another. In such cases, we need to perform the integration of data horizontally.

Suppose we already have two datasets from different sources, viz. `city_general_info` and `city_demographics_info`. `city_general_info` is a list of dictionaries containing the following information about each city: *city_id, state, country,* and *area*. `city_demographics_info` is a list of dictionaries containing the following information about each city: *city_id, demonym, official_languages,* and *popular_cuisine*. Then, for the final dataset to have all the attributes, we would need to combine all the information based on the *CityID*. The process would look something as follows:

```
import random
from copy import deepcopy

city_general_info = {'987654': {'name': 'Delhi',
'country': 'India', ...}, '123456': {'name':
'San Francisco', 'country': 'United States of
America', ...}}
city_demographics_info = {'987654': {'demonym':
```

```
'Delhiite', ...}, '123456': {'demonym': 'San
Franciscan', ...}}
merged_data = []

for city_id in city_general_info:
    temp_dict = deepcopy(city_general_info[city_
id])
    temp_dict.update({'city_id': city_id})
    if city_id in city_demographics_info:
      temp_dict.update(city_demographics_
info[city_id])
    merged_data.append(temp_dict)


random.shuffle(merged_data)
```

5 • DATA TRANSFORMATION

Presently, there is so much content available on the web that
it is impossible to check the correctness of all. The content
posted by the publisher, like the product name, product sizing,
and product description, may have been moderated to some
extent. However, the user's content, like the review of product
quality and fit, body measurements, which we are blatantly
using to feed into the model, could likely be noisy. Therefore,
it is necessary to scrub the dataset using specific techniques to
produce a quality dataset, and the process is known as *Data
Transformation*.

Datasets for problems like *Size Recommendation* may involve
parsing users' reviews to extract relevant feedback on the fit
as an additional feature. The inconsistencies in the text, in this
case, can be easily removed using some straightforward string
transformations. Data Transformation's primary focus is to
scrub the dataset's raw values to remove redundancies and
correct the language and logical semantics.

The process mentioned above is significantly different from the transformation in the *Data Preprocessing* pipeline that involves further mutating these scrubbed values into formats easily understandable by the model. As a distinction example, transforming a string to correct the spell errors would form a part of the Data Transformation process. In contrast, encoding the updated string into a *bag of words (BoW)* representation would be part of Data Preprocessing. Worry not, as we shall talk in detail about Data Preprocessing later in the book! For now, read on the few suggestions we have for some quick transformations:

• When users leave a product review, they can write a text with multiple special characters and emojis. Encoding such characters may require extra effort. We would have to convert these emojis into their *Unicode* representation before feeding them as input to our model. If we had some sentiment analysis tasks, such encoding would have helped tremendously. However, in the case of fit feedback, they might not provide umpteen useful signals. Thus, we can remove them and use plain text only. The following example uses Python's *Regular Expression (RegEx)* library's *substitute* method to do such processing:

```
import re
def preprocess_review(review):
    return re.sub(r"[^a-zA-Z0-9\s]+", ' ', review)
```

In the *preprocess_review* method above, we are replacing every character that is not alphanumeric or Unicode whitespaces (which include \t, \n, \r, \f, and \v) with the simple whitespace character. This processing reduces the string's complexity and helps the algorithm focus on the critical pieces regarding the fit feedback.

```
INPUT:
"heyy!!! I am Cr@zi-@**-St@# !
welcome aboard , love this website <3
purchased this dress, fit perfectly 1000000%%%%
will I buy this again??? #eLL Ye$$$"

OUTPUT:
"heyy    I am Cr zi      St
welcome aboard   love this website  3
purchased this dress  fit perfectly 1000000
will I buy this again      eLL Ye    "
```

- Users seldom take care of grammar, spellings, and sentence formation when they leave a product review on online platforms. It is highly probable that a user might misspell some words that would ultimately impact the Machine Learning model's performance. Thus, a quick way to improve the dataset's quality would be to use some Python libraries to perform spell-check.

```python
from spellchecker import SpellChecker

spellChecker = SpellChecker()

def spellcheck_review(review):
  words = review.split()
  corrected_words = []
  for word in words:
    corrected_words.append(spellChecker.
correction(word))
  return ' '.join(corrected_words)
```

```
INPUT:
"heyy!!! I am Cr@zyStacie !
wlecome aboard , love this webste <3
purchsaed this amzing dress, and it fit perfctly
1000000%%%%
will I buy this agian??? #eLL Ye$$$"

OUTPUT:
"heyy!!! I am Cr@zyStacie !
welcome aboard , love this webster a3
purchased this amazing dress, and it fit
perfectly 1000000%%%%
will I buy this again??? well Ye$$$"
```

The above example uses Python's *PySpellChecker* library to correct the spell errors. If required, we can go one step further by using libraries like *NLPre* to do more sophisticated checks to smooth some of the more tricky inconsistencies found in real-world data.

6• DATA BALANCING

We can segregate the records into different groups or classes based on their label value in a dataset. For example, each category in the *News Category* dataset, like *sports*, *politics*, *entertainment*, and *community*, can have multiple records. Similarly, in the *Sarcasm Detection* dataset, we can classify the records as either *sarcastic* or *non-sarcastic*. Typically, the volume of different classes is not the same. The learning algorithms can handle some differences in class distribution (say $2:3$); however, the problem arises when the differences become extreme (say $1:99$). We refer to datasets with extremely skewed class distribution as an *Imbalanced Dataset*.

Let us try to understand how the learning algorithm works under class imbalance for a binary classification scenario, where the model assigns a weight to each class. The class with a sizable record volume in the dataset is known as the *majority class*, whereas the other is the *minority class*. The abundance of majority class could impact the model's predictive capability if not handled correctly. In extreme cases, the model learns to completely ignore the minority class by not giving them any weight. We can detect this skewed behavior of the classification model by an evaluation metric called the *Confusion Matrix*. There are different ways to handle imbalanced datasets; let us walk through them.

I• ELIMINATING INFREQUENT DATA RECORDS

This technique is only applicable to cases where the dataset has multiple classes, and no particular class has to be necessarily present to solve the problem at hand. For example, the *Clothing Fit* dataset has only three classes: *small*, *fit*, and *large*, and all of them are essential to address the *Size Recommendation* problem. Whereas in the *News Category* dataset, we have many available classes like *sports*, *politics*, *entertainment*, *fashion*, *medicine*, and *community*. We do not have strict requirements for any particular class's presence to address the *News Category Detection* problem.

A straightforward way to tackle the extreme skewness is to remove records of very infrequent classes from the dataset. We can also consider going the other route of dropping the records of frequent classes to match the proportion of infrequent classes; however, it may significantly slash down the dataset's size. The former approach looks more reasonable here as it maintains the data volume and would help the model classify reliably.

In the *News Category* dataset extracted from *HuffPost*, we performed preliminary *Exploratory Data Analysis (EDA)*. We found that there were a few categories with less than 500 articles listed under them. To balance the dataset, we merely removed them and saw an increase in the classification model's performance.

```
import json
from collections import defaultdict

category_count = defaultdict(int)
for record in data:
  category_count[record['category']] += 1

filtered_data = []
for record in data:
  if category_count[record['category']] >= 500:
    filtered_data.append(record)

output_file = open('./News_Category_Dataset.
json','w',encoding='utf-8')
for record in filtered_data:
  output_file.write(json.dumps(record) + '\n')
output_file.close()
```

II• RANDOMLY SAMPLING DATA RECORDS

Sampling is an extensively popular and uncomplicated approach to deal with imbalanced datasets. This technique entails randomly sampling records from the abundant classes in the dataset to remove the skewness, a process often called *Random Undersampling*. As an alternate, we can also randomly sample with replacement to increase the records for infrequent classes, also known as *Random Oversampling*.

In the *Sarcasm Detection* dataset, we extracted sarcastic headlines from *TheOnion* and real-world news headlines from *HuffPost*. The statistics show that non-sarcastic news headlines (~200k) are a lot more than the sarcastic headlines (~11k). To remove the skewness in this case, we use the undersampling technique: we randomly sampled ~15k headlines from non-sarcastic data. It is important to note that we do not always aim to have a 1:1 ratio for the classes; as discussed previously slight skewness, like 2:3, can be handled effectively by learning algorithms.

```
data = deepcopy(sarcastic_data)

random.shuffle(non_sarcastic_data)

for i in range(0, 15000):
  hh = preprocess_headline(non_sarcastic_data[i]
['headline'])
  if len(hh.split()) > 1:
    temp = dict()
    temp['is_sarcastic'] = 0
    temp['headline'] = hh
    temp['article_link'] = non_sarcastic_data[i]
['link']
    data.append(temp)
```

III • ASSIGNING CLASS WEIGHTS

Weighing parameters is a fundamental concept in Machine Learning, which depicts how much significance a particular entity holds. Weights could be related to a specific feature, a specific data record, or a neuron in an artificial neural network. In imbalanced datasets, we can assign the records of infrequent classes more weight than records from frequent classes. This step makes the learning algorithm penalize the misprediction on infrequent classes more, which compensates for the limited signal they provide due to less quantity.

For example, consider a dataset of 1M loan records, where the label indicates if the loanee repaid it on time or not. Assuming only 0.01 % of people do not pay off loans on time, we have 999k records of timely payments (say, label = 1) as the *majority* class and the rest 1k as the *minority* class (say, label = 0). In this case, we can use the rudimentary method of assigning the class weights inversely proportional to their respective frequencies, i.e., $w_i = N/(C*n_i)$. Here, w_i is the ith class's weight, N is the total number of records in the dataset, C is the total number of classes, and n_i is the number of records in the dataset belonging to the ith class. Using this technique, we find that the records with timely payments are assigned a weight of *0.5* owing to their higher frequency, whereas the other class gets assigned a value of *500*! This would mean that the misclassification of the latter class would be penalized *1000* times more than the former.

IV• PICKING CORRECT EVALUATION METRIC

When working with even slightly disproportionate datasets, it is necessary to pick a relevant evaluation metric to assess the model's performance effectively. *Accuracy* may not always be the best metric. Consider the model which predicts *if an alien would land on earth in the next 24 hours*. Undoubtedly the model would forecast *'no'* as the answer with an accuracy rate of 99.99%, indicating that the model is highly accurate. However, in actuality, the model might not be usable if it cannot accurately predict records with *'yes'* as an answer.

In cases like these, the *F1 Score* might be a more relevant metric which we could consider. In the statistical analysis of classification problems, the F1 Score is the harmonic mean of the model's *precision* and *recall* values. It ranges from 0 to 1 and denotes perfect precision and recall at the value 1. However, the drawback is that it is defined only for a particular classification threshold (often 0.5 is the default value for a binary classification scenario). This threshold usually needs some tuning, specifically in cases where we have a data imbalance issue. A better metric for such cases is the *Precision-Recall Area Under the Curve (PR-AUC)*, which is the area under the precision-recall curve produced by varying the classification thresholds. PR-AUC can also be thought of as the average of the precision scores calculated for each recall threshold.

V • Alter Problem Definition

This approach is one of the most interesting to deal with highly imbalanced datasets (where the minority class may occur only 1 in 1000 records). So far, we have been viewing the problems as simple classification where we train the model to intelligently categorize data records into groups, be it in majority class or minority class. We observed that simple classification learning algorithms have trouble by skewed datasets as majority classes cloud the characteristics of minority classes and disrupt the model's predictive capability. Hence, it would be smart to alter the problem definition and view it from an angle of *Anomaly Detection*. Anomaly Detection is the type of problem where the task is to identify unusual points in the dataset, i.e., occurrences that are *different* (here they could be minority class) from the *regular* (majority class in our case) ones. This technique is often called *Outlier Detection*. Modifying our problem interpretation, in this case, helps us use the imbalanced datasets without amending their composition.

7 • Data Exporting

After we have done all the tedious tasks of scrubbing, trimming, and balancing the data, the final task is to export and release it to the public. It is crucial to choose an appropriate structure and a suitable format to export the datasets. A dataset is more likely to be accessed, used, and shared by more people if it has an uncomplicated structure and is in an easy-to-use format to import in different learning frameworks. The manageability of the dataset is another essential characteristic. It assists in the trouble-free existence of the data in the system for extended periods and fuels innovation.

We can consider different structures to express a dataset appropriately, the key ones being the following:

- *Tabular*: This is the most common structure where we organize data into rows of data records and columns listing records' attributes. It is best suited for independent records of data and can be effectively exported in CSV formats.

- *Hierarchical*: These data structures support sets where data records are linked to other data records in a vertical tree composition. That is, the attributes themselves might be key-value pairs. Hierarchical data structures are functionally exported in JSON formats.

- *Network*: In this data structure, multiple associations exist between the different data records, just like a spider web or a social network.

We can also quickly discuss different formats we can use to export a dataset into:

- *Comma-Separated Values (CSV)*: As discussed previously, this format is highly effective for tabular datasets, to put simply, rows and columns. A new line separates each data record, and a comma (,) separates the attributes in a single data record. The first row should always be the header row, which indicates the names of the attributes that follow. It looks something like the following:

```
username,pin,first_name,last_name
heylaura,1234,Laura,Wu
iampc,999,Paige,Carter
... ... ...
```

CSV files are saved with a `.csv` extension. CSV files have a handful of advantages as they are easy to skim by the human eye and simple to implement and parse. They are trouble-free to import and manipulate the data. The data is faster to handle and offers a compact version. However, it supports only basic types and creates a parsing ruckus if the attributes' values contain commas themselves. It does not support special characters and has no universal standard.

• **Tab-Separated Values (TSV):** This format is pretty similar to CSV but instead of commas uses tabs (or \t) to separate attribute values in a single record. TSV is an alternative to the common CSV, mainly because having commas in attribute values (say textual data) is very common, causing issues during parsing, but tabs are unusual. The files are then saved with a `.tsv` extension and look something like the following:

```
username    pin     first_name    last_name
heylaura    1234    Laura         Wu
iampc       999     Paige         Carter
...         ...     ...
```

• **JavaScript Object Notation (JSON):** Previously, we discussed how hierarchical data is best suited for JSON format as it allows the transmission of tree-like data in a human-readable format. It nests multiple key-value pairs as a dictionary and is independent of the data type or the programming language used. JSON syntax is both easy and fast to read and parse. It supports nested schema and makes manipulation of data structure effortless in comparison to other formats. The corresponding files are saved with a .json extension and look something like the following:

```
[
    {
        "username": "heylaura",
        "pin": 1234,
        "first_name": "Laura",
        "last_name": "Wu"
    },
    {
        "username": "iampc",
        "pin": 999,
        "first_name": "Paige",
        "last_name": "Carter"
    },
    ... ... ...
]
```

- **Extensible Markup Language (XML)**: Datasets exported in this markup language as .xml files are in a format easily readable by both humans and machines. XML is used mostly for textual data for its strong support of multiple languages via *Unicode*. Though XML might be easy to use and generalize, it is very verbose, thus bloating up the volume, and is not used widely for exporting datasets.

```
<?xml version="1.0" encoding="UTF-8"?>
<root>
  <row>
```

```
    <username>heylaura</username>
    <pin>1234</pin>
    <first_name>Laura</first_name>
    <last_name>Wu</last_name>
  </row>
  <row>
    <username>iampc</username>
    <pin>999</pin>
    <first_name>Paige</first_name>
    <last_name>Carter</last_name>
  </row>

  ... ... ...
</root>
```

There are other formats in which datasets are seldom exported like HTML (.*html*), Spreadsheets (.*xls*, .*ods*, or .*gsheet*), *Statistical Product and Service Solutions (SPSS)* (.*dat* or .*sps*), and so on. However, CSV and JSON are the two most popular formats for exporting and importing datasets because of all their positive points.

If we recall, we have been dealing with hierarchical data structure throughout with data extracted from *ModCloth*. For simplicity, we can export all of that into a JSON format.

```
import json

output_file = open('./ModCloth_scraped_data.json',
'w',encoding='utf-8')
for r in scraped_data:
  output_file.write(json.dumps(r) + '\n')
output_file.close()
```

The exported dataset can then be imported into a learning framework as follows:

```
def parseJson(fname):
  for line in open(fname, 'r'):
    yield eval(line)

scraped_data = list(parseJson('./ModCloth_scraped_
data.json'))
```

CHAPTER 4

DATASET PREPROCESSING & FEATURE ENGINEERING

In the previous chapter, we learned about various steps to scrub the raw data we extracted and structure it so that other folks can use the dataset to address various challenges. One of the straightforward ways to utilize the dataset is to feed it into a Machine Learning pipeline; however, that might not be very effective. Before we use the data for training a model, we might need to go through a few more steps to make it suitable for the model's understanding instead of the human understanding we aimed at previously.

Data Preprocessing and *Feature Engineering* are the two fundamental processes that precede training a model in the Machine Learning pipeline. Both the processes depend greatly on the dataset we are using, the learning algorithm's requirements, the domain of the problem, and many other such factors. It is thus vital to understand the basics of the various methodologies covered under these umbrellas.

DATA PREPROCESSING

In the *Clothing Fit* dataset extracted from *ModCloth*, we had attributes like *'length'*: *'just right'* and *'original_size'*: *'xxxl'*. Undoubtedly, these are valuable pieces of information, which indicate important aspects of the product proportions. Humans easily understand these values; however, a Machine Learning model might have trouble learning from this type of data. Encoding the data in machine-understandable form might work better.

Furthermore, data extraction processes are not as tightly controlled in terms of quality, leading to some outliers. For example, having an entry as *original_size'*: *'q'*, or having weird data combinations, like *'height'*: *'100m'* and *'waist'*: *'25cm'*. These erratic and whimsical data points make pattern discovery difficult for a model, thus needing handling before using the dataset.

To combat these shortcomings, we need to overhaul our datasets' attributes to fill the gaps, address inconsistencies, and represent data in a suitable format for the Machine Learning model to work. This process is referred to as *Data Preprocessing*. Let us go over some frequently used data preprocessing techniques.

1 • VECTORIZATION

Machine Learning models are mathematical models that expect input data to be in numerical format. To that end, data attributes that are not in the form of numbers (or set of numbers) need to be transformed before we can train a Machine Learning model. The process of converting features into a suitable numerical form is known as *Vectorization*. This step is mandatory for data preprocessing and involves transforming all kinds of non-numeric data viz. textual, graphical, and categorical, to a numeric form. In this section, we shall be talking about Text Vectorization, Image Vectorization, and Categorical Vectorization with a few examples.

I• TEXT VECTORIZATION

As per the overview, *Text Vectorization* involves transforming the text into something a machine can understand, like a vector (or an array) of real numbers. This step is essential for doing a language-aware analysis.

One of the primary methods of vectorizing a text is the *Bag-of-Words (BoW)* technique, which assumes that the text's meaning and similarity are encoded in the *word vocabulary*. Given a block of text containing multiple sentences, BoW creates a *word vocabulary* containing all the text's distinct words. It then creates a vector of length equal to that of the vocabulary's and assigns a score to each word's position to denote the word's contribution to the text. There are multiple ways of computing the score of a word:

- *Word Count:* Total number of occurrences of a word in the text.

- *Word Frequency:* Total number of occurrences of a word in the text divided by the total number of words in the text.

- *Term Frequency–Inverse Document Frequency (TF-IDF):* The importance of a word in the text is computed based on the concept that words that frequently occur in certain documents are more important than the words that frequently occur in general.

Let us look at an example to observe how the sturdy yet straightforward word count BoW technique works. Let us assume we have the following word vocabulary consisting of unique lower-case words from all the review texts:

```
word_vocabulary = { outfit, shirt, blouse, bottom,
jeans, pants, skirt, dress, love, hate, favorite,
trash, yes, no, me, i, mine, my, this, that }
```

Using the BoW technique, we can represent the review *"I love this dress, my favorite dress"* as the following vector:

```
"I love this dress, my favorite dress" → [0,0,0,
0,0,0,0,2,1,0,0,0,0,0,0,1,0,0,1,0]
```

The representation is also known as an *Embedding*. We can further improve the representations using the following techniques:

1. We can filter out common words that provide no insight into the semantic of the text. In the *Natural Language Processing (NLP)* world, such words are called *stop words*. The following is a list of stop words from the English language defined in the *Natural Language Toolkit (NLTK)*.

```
{'ourselves', 'hers', 'between', 'yourself',
'but', 'again', 'there', 'about', 'once',
'during', 'out', 'very', 'having', 'with',
```

```
'they', 'own', 'an', 'be', 'some', 'for',
'do', 'its', 'yours', 'such', 'into', 'of',
'most', 'itself', 'other', 'off', 'is', 's',
'am', 'or', 'who', 'as', 'from', 'him',
'each', 'the', 'themselves', 'until',
'below', 'are', 'we', 'these', 'your', 'his',
'through', 'don', 'nor', 'me', 'were', 'her',
'more', 'himself', 'this', 'down', 'should',
'our', 'their', 'while', 'above', 'both',
'up', 'to', 'ours', 'had', 'she', 'all',
'no', 'when', 'at', 'any', 'before', 'them',
'same', 'and', 'been', 'have', 'in', 'will',
'on', 'does', 'yourselves', 'then', 'that',
'because', 'what', 'over', 'why', 'so',
'can', 'did', 'not', 'now', 'under', 'he',
'you', 'herself', 'has', 'just', 'where',
'too', 'only', 'myself', 'which', 'those',
'i', 'after', 'few', 'whom', 't', 'being',
'if', 'theirs', 'my', 'against', 'a', 'by',
'doing', 'it', 'how', 'further', 'was',
'here', 'than'}
```

2. We can shrink the vocabulary size by reducing the derived words to their base form or the stem word, a process known as *Stemming*. This technique is often seen when we search for a particular keyword on a search engine and it returns results containing its derived words. It is worth noting that the stem word may not necessarily be the morphological root of the word.

Stemming is a crude method for cataloging words related to each other and is usually done by chopping off from the end until we reach the word's stem. For example, stemming the following words: *'fit'*, *'fitter'*, *'fitted'*, *'fitting'*, *'fittable'*, *'fittest'* to their stem word *'fit'* helps convey almost the same meaning but with a reduced vocabulary. Though this chopping off approach works well in many cases, it leads to many exceptions, especially in a language like English. For this, we have other sophisticated techniques like Porter Algorithm, Snowball Algorithm, and so on.

3. We can continue with the above process of shrinking the vocabulary size by reducing the derived words to their base form, where the base form is the word's morphological root, a process known as *Lemmatization*. Lemmatization looks beyond just chopping off the word and relies on the lexical meaning to obtain the correct base form, thus giving a much more informative view. For example, lemmatization would reduce the following words *'be'*, *'been'*, *'being'*, *'was'* with its lemma, i.e., *'be'*.

4. We can count the occurrences of a sequence of words rather than individual words. This technique is more useful than counting individual words since the meaning of a word depends heavily on the context in which it is being used. In statistical language models, a sequence of n words is called an *n-gram*. N-grams find their applications in areas like auto-completion of sentences and spell-check.

The above count-based approaches help generate a sturdy embedding for text vectorization; however, they do not capture the text's exact semantic meaning with utmost sophistication. Hence, it is worthwhile to explore advanced techniques using *Recurrent Neural Networks (RNN)* to fabricate complex contextual text embeddings.

II• IMAGE VECTORIZATION

Playing around with images, we start to see individual *pixels* (as below) when we zoom in on an image. These pixels are nothing but individual elements of a picture, a basic unit of programmable color for a digital image. Hence, an image represents pixels in a grid form, each having its color.

As we zoom in on the image, we begin
to see the individual pixels.

In the rainbow world, each pixel gets its color through a combination of the three primary colors: *Red* (R), *Green* (G), and *Blue* (B). Therefore, in mathematical terms, each pixel in the image can be represented by three different numbers, indicating each of RGB pigments' intensity with 256 levels each. For example, a *crimson* pixel can be represented as `RGB(220,20,60)`.

We can apply the above knowledge to convert a pixel-based image into a vector-based image containing only numbers for the model to comprehend. A high-resolution colored PNG image of dimensions say `1028*768 px` can be an input to the model as a 3-dimensional vector of size `1028*768*3`. For a *grayscale* image, we can represent each pixel with a single value, indicating the white color intensity. `0` denotes *black* pixel value, `255` denotes *white*, and the numbers between denoting different gray shades. The grayscale image can thus be vectorized as a 2-dimensional vector of size `1028*768` instead. This pixel-based approach is one of the most straightforward techniques to vectorize an image. There are other ways like *Color Histogram Vectorization* that we could experiment with depending on the use case and our problem's complexity.

III • Categorical Vectorization

When we look into the *Clothing Fit* dataset's product sizing column, we observe that the values always belong to a specific set, viz. *XXS*, *XS*, *S*, *M*, *L*, *XL*, and *XXL*. We would need to vectorize these categories and encode them as numeric values before feeding it to a model. Let us talk about the different ways we can encode this categorical column of our dataset.

A • Integer Encoding

One of the easiest methods would be to assign each category (or product size in this case) a unique numeric value, something as below.

XXS	1
XS	2
S	3
M	4
L	5
XL	6
XXL	7

The integer assignments follow a natural ordering similar to their corresponding sizes. This encoding aids the model to understand that size *XXS* is close to *S* compared to size *XL* (since 1 is closer to 3 than 6). One fine print with this method is that it only works when there is a natural ordering between the categorical values. If we have an encoding like `{S:1, M:2, L:3, XS:4, XL:5, XXS:6, XXL:7}`, it might not work. Hence, it is essential to wisely encode categorical values, as incorrect assignments could lead to unexpected results.

B• One-Hot Encoding

For categorical features, where no ordinal relationship exists, the above-defined *Integer Encoding* might be overkill or not work at all. In situations like these, we use a widely popular and creative way to encode the categories in a binary form called the *One-Hot Encoding*. It represents each value as a binary vector of a size equivalent to the number of possible categorical values. Only the value assumed in the respective data records is turned on or assigned *1*, and the rest are turned off or assigned *0*. For example, if all the product sizes are *{XXS, XS, S, M, L, XL, XXL}*, then we can do the encoding of the different product sizes like the following:

```
XXS        [1,0,0,0,0,0,0]
XS         [0,1,0,0,0,0,0]
S          [0,0,1,0,0,0,0]
M          [0,0,0,1,0,0,0]
L          [0,0,0,0,1,0,0]
XL         [0,0,0,0,0,1,0]
XXL        [0,0,0,0,0,0,1]
```

This way of encoding could be easily adapted to new possible inputs. For example, let us say *ModCloth* introduces new product sizes as *PS, PM,* and *PL* for petite body types. In this case, we can extend the existing vectors by appending three additional zeros and introduce encodings for the new sizes by using these additional 3 bits, which looks something like the following:

```
XXS        [1,0,0,0,0,0,0,0,0,0]
XS         [0,1,0,0,0,0,0,0,0,0]
S          [0,0,1,0,0,0,0,0,0,0]
M          [0,0,0,1,0,0,0,0,0,0]
L          [0,0,0,0,1,0,0,0,0,0]
XL         [0,0,0,0,0,1,0,0,0,0]
XXL        [0,0,0,0,0,0,1,0,0,0]
PS         [0,0,0,0,0,0,0,1,0,0]
PM         [0,0,0,0,0,0,0,0,1,0]
PL         [0,0,0,0,0,0,0,0,0,1]
```

2• NORMALIZATION

Recall the example of the *World Cities* dataset we discussed in the previous chapter, which had an attribute indicating each city's population. Logically, the values in this column could range anything in between 1 (*Monowi, Nebraska boasts of having only a single resident! Unbelievable, right?*) to a couple of millions. Training on this dataset could lead to getting stuck with NaNs as the gradient update becomes too large to handle owing to the vast range in values.

Now consider the *average age* of the population as an attribute. The values of this column would mainly lie between 0 and 100. This range is quite different from that of the *population*. Training a Machine Learning model with these two attributes in the dataset would make the gradient bounce rapidly because of the two different scales, thus slowing down the convergence process. Many times, optimizers like *AdaGrad* or *Adam* are used to guard against this problem by creating a different learning rate per feature. However, optimizers may not always save us from all problems, especially when each feature has a wide range of values.

To combat the above problems, we should transform the values of the features belonging to varied scales and bring them on a similar scale without changing their original behavior, a process referred to as *Normalization*. In more complex scenarios, normalization also refers to sophisticated adjustments to shepherd the entire probability distributions of adjusted values into alignment. Normalization helps improve the numeric stability of the model by aiding the gradient to ascent (or descent) with a decent speed rather than taking too large (thus bouncing back and forth) or too small (thus never converging) jumps. This behavior further helps in speeding up the training speed of the model.

There are multiple ways to calibrate the feature distributions;

let us discuss the four most common ones.

I • Feature Clipping

If we plot the population of all the cities in the world from the *World Cities* dataset, we would observe the graph has long tails on both sides probably. The cities with significantly less population (imagine the number of cities with only a single resident or less than ten even!) and those with a vast population would practically be outliers. In such cases, we can set a minimum and maximum population (say set a range from 2,000 to 20,000,000) and clip the outliers. We set values less than the minimum to the minimum value and values greater than the maximum to the maximum value. This technique is called *Feature Clipping*.

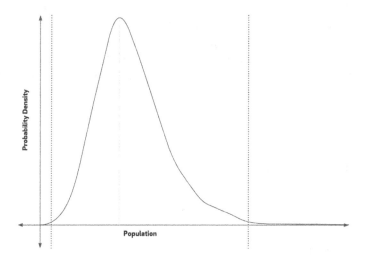

A probability density plot of the population of different cities. Conceptually, the extremes ends can be clipped off.

A sophisticated way to find the minimum and maximum of the feature values is to use the measure of standard deviation, for example, clipping the values beyond the range of (-nσ, +nσ). Feature Clipping is a simple yet effective way of normalizing the data. The most significant advantage is that it can be applied before or after other normalization techniques.

II • RANGE SCALING

Consider the age feature in the *World Cities* dataset that can have a definite range from 0 to 100 years after clipping. Each age value has a substantial number of people. We can fix the upper, and the lower bounds of the feature distribution as the probability of outliers is low (*only 0.0173% of Americans live to 100!*). In such cases, *Range Scaling* is an effective way of normalization. This technique mutates the feature values from their existing range, here [0, 100], to a standard range, which is usually [0, 1] or [-1, 1]. This approach is also known as the *Min-Max Scaling* because of the way we transform the ranges. The following defines the formula to rescale to a range of [0, 1], where x' represents the transformed value, and x is the feature's original value. min(x) and max(x) represent the lower and the upper bounds of the original range.

$$x' = \frac{x - min(x)}{max(x) - min(x)}$$

The following is a generalized formula that can be used to rescale to an arbitrary range [p, q]:

$$x' = p + \frac{(x - min(x))(q - p)}{max(x) - min(x)}$$

III • LOG SCALING

Observe the *number of languages spoken* feature in the *World Cities* dataset; we see that it follows a *power-law distribution*. To put it in simpler words, a handful of languages cover most cities, while the rest cover only the remaining few. Though this distribution represents the data accurately, it does not gel well with the model training process. To work with skewed distributions like these, we use *Log Scaling*, which transforms the distribution into a normal distribution. Log Scaling narrows down the original range of the feature values by performing a log transform over all the values, something like below (where x is the original value and x' is the transformed value):

$$x' = log(x)$$

Log Scaling compresses a wide range to a narrow range and reduces the variability of the data generically. This transformation helps in improving the performance of the learning algorithm. The outliers might cause the log-transformed distributions to be still a bit skewed and not entirely normal. However, they are closer to being normally distributed as compared to the original distribution.

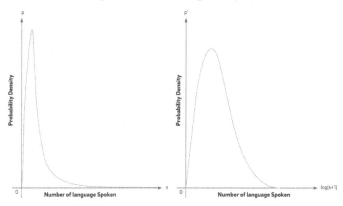

A probability density plot of the number of languages spoken in different cities (*left*). Noticeably, the plot with log scaling (*right*) helps in reducing the skewness of data.

IV• Z-Score Scaling

When a feature value distribution contains only a few outliers where feature clipping might not yield drastic changes, we tend to use the *Z-Score Scaling* technique. This normalization method transforms the data by converting the values to a common scale with a mean value of 0 and a standard deviation value of 1.

In statistics, *Z-Score* is a metric that quantifies a value's relationship to the *mean (μ)* of the entire group in terms of the number of *standard deviations (σ)*. For instance, if the value is equal to the mean of the group, Z-Score would be 0. The following is used to compute the transformed value (or the Z-Score) denoted by x' from the original value x:

$$x' = \frac{x - \mu}{\sigma}$$

The above described the four widely popular techniques to normalize the data. However, it is up to us to choose the appropriate approach based on the use case, learning algorithm, and data distribution. Regardless of the technique we use, our data should have the following characteristics for the model to perform well:

- *Slender Range:* This indicates that the range of the feature values should be barely sufficient to accurately represent the distribution. As a standard, many data practitioners like to rescale feature values in the range *[0,1]* or *[-1,1]*.

- *Homogeneity:* This requires different feature columns in the dataset to follow near-calibrated ranges or lie in similar feature value ranges.

3 • BUCKETIZATION

When a dataset constitutes observations from a survey or an experiment, it ought to have some discrepancies. Hence to reduce the effects of those minor observation errors, we use a technique called *Bucketization*. This approach involves replacing the original values with the value of the respective bin. Mapping of feature values to bins can be done by defining small intervals on a continuous scale (based on some thresholds), and the process is called *Data Binning*. Aggregating numeric values is associated with loss of information at times; however, it reduces the amount of data to be processed. It thereby eases the model's training without any drastic performance changes. It also reduces the impact of noise, for example, in Image Processing problems.

I • SYMMETRIC BUCKETIZATION

In this approach of *Symmetric Bucketization*, we divide the entire feature value range into equal-sized intervals. The thresholds are identically spaced, with fixed boundaries for each interval. This type of binning is useful when the feature values are uniformly distributed across the entire range. However, suppose the feature values are not uniformly distributed. In that case, certain buckets might have an extremely high number of points, and others may have very few or even none, thus leading to an imbalance. Therefore, it is essential to ensure the uniform distributions of the feature values before applying this technique as it might hinder the learning.

II • QUANTILE BUCKETIZATION

Quantile Bucketization aims to cover the shortcomings of the above-defined Symmetric Bucketization. It smartly creates buckets, or bins, having an equal number of points within them. In statistics, *quantiles* are cut points that divide the entire distribution into groups such that they contain the same fraction of the total population. Based on this concept, the thresholds are not equally-spaced through the whole range of the feature values. Instead, they are governed by the number of data points lying between any two, which should be equal for all. By this logic, there would be more bins (with smaller size) in the area with higher data density, and less bins (with larger size) in the areas where data is more spread out. Therefore, Quantile Bucketization is preferred when the data distribution is skewed since it is adaptive and mimics the original distribution closely.

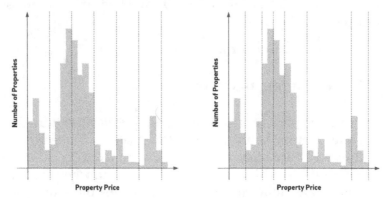

A side-by-side comparison of the symmetric and quantile style of binning.

FEATURE ENGINEERING

After data preprocessing, we can use the data to train a Machine Learning model and deploy it in production to work on unseen data. This simple model has the obvious set of features, usually mirroring the dataset's attributes, and could perform reasonably well in addressing the problem at hand. To further improve the model's performance, we have two choices:

1. Model Iteration: One approach is to iterate on building sophisticated Machine Learning models, for instance, by increasing the number of hidden layers in a neural network or taking an ensemble of different types of models with the hope to learn more effectively. Using multiple Machine

Learning models in conjugation to obtain better predictive performance is referred to as *Ensemble Learning*. This action plan might yield the desired results; however, it requires much time and effort to develop and comes with a risk of not working entirely despite all the efforts. It also necessitates a larger volume of training data that comes with another risk of models not scaling to production traffic.

2. *Feature Iteration*: The other course of action is to engineer new and better features. The features mirror the structure of the data, which are identifiable even by the sub-optimal models. Thus, having a better representation of data influences the predictive models' performance. The process of *Feature Engineering* identifies features that might provide additional signals to our existing model to improve its performance. Constructing features is an exciting aspect where all the intuition, creativity, and black art happens. Andrew Ng says that *"Coming up with features is difficult, time-consuming, and requires expert knowledge. Applied machine learning is basically feature engineering in itself"*. With this approach, we can keep the simple model in production, which further reduces the risk of failure in terms of scalability and performance.

As we start our journey to address a real-world problem with Machine Learning, it makes sense to aim for low hanging fruits. Weighing the pros and cons of the two approaches, we should first focus on engineering better features to quickly boost the performance before moving on to more challenging and risky tasks. With innovative features in our basket, we can avert from using complex ensemble learning techniques or spend eternities searching for the best model parameters, a process known as *Hyperparameter Tuning*.

Furthermore, experimenting with new features improves our understanding of how the model reacts to new information and addresses our problem more aptly. However, this only works within a limit until we have explored all possibilities. We would not like to go overboard with *'feature over-engineering'*, thus ending up with unwieldy dimensions (which we shall discuss later in this chapter).

WHAT IS NOT FEATURE ENGINEERING?

Before we dive deep into the different subtasks of Feature Engineering, which will help us in creating an exhaustive list of features for model training, it is necessary to paint a clearer picture by pausing and highlighting what is *not* feature engineering:

- It does not include identifying the data signals present in the dataset while gathering data from a source.

- It does not subsume spotting the target variable or the label of each data record in the train or test set.

- It does not cover the process of data cleansing, with tasks like removing punctuations and stop words or curating word embeddings.

- It also does not encompass processing the data by scaling the values to a particular range, normalizing the values, encoding categorical values, and so on.

THE ITERATIVE PROCESS

Understanding the process of feature engineering as an applied Machine Learning task highlights that it does not stand-alone. It is an iterative process with a well-defined problem that oscillates between feature ideation and model evaluation till we hit a plateau. Once that happens, we can then play around with complex model architecture or hyperparameter tuning. The step-by-step process followed in a formal setting for feature engineering usually looks like this:

1. Understanding the problem statement and the domain to brainstorm ideas for new features by analyzing recent trends

and discussing with experts.

2. Extracting the feature values for offline statistical analysis after some transformations.

3. Training the existing model on data including new features and *analyzing the model performance metrics*.

4. In case the feature does not give a performance boost, we can try different transformation ideas or simply go back to brainstorming other features. Otherwise, we further work on getting the feature *productionized*, thereby integrating it with the model serving pipeline. For more context, *model serving* is an approach of exposing the trained model as an endpoint to which we simply feed our data and get prediction results.

FEATURE TYPES

Modern Machine Learning models are data-hungry, but the fundamental aspect is feeding the data in the right format. Passing on raw features in the data might make the model training slower. They impede the generalization power of the model and impact the performance negatively. It is essential to understand that the features' data type significantly influences the processing approach. Following we give a brief overview of the four types of commonly used features:

1. Continuous Features: A continuous feature can assume any real number, including floats. There is no definite boundary between any two feature values, i.e., there could be infinitely many possible values lying between those two. These feature values are essentially numeric and hence can be performed mathematical operations on. For example, the products on *ModCloth* have prices like *US$14.99, US$25.00, US$99.99*, and so on. Moreover, there is no strict distinction between partitions (unlike other types we shall study below), i.e., a product could even be listed for *US$15.10*, and that would work too!

2. Binary Features: These are one of the simplest types of features and can only have one of the two possible values: *1* or *0, true* or *false, on* or *off, yes* or *no,* and so on. These kinds of dichotomous features are easy to experiment with, as they do not require fancy transformations. For instance, we can denote if a user on *ModCloth* is *verified* or *not verified.* A potential scenario would be that the model learns to assign more weight to reviews of verified users than their counterparts.

3. String Features: The values of a string feature can assume any block of text, be it alphabets, symbols, or emojis. As we discussed previously, these string features need processing and should be converted to a vector of numeric values. The obvious example of this would be the review text of any product as left by the user, like *"I love this dress, it is my favorite. The size first me perfectly and flatters my curves!"*

4. Discrete Features: These features are also commonly referred to as *Categorical Features*. The discrete feature values can assume only one of the N possible values and have definite boundaries between them. In simpler terms, there could be no other value in between the pre-defined N values to which they can be assigned. A point to be noted is that there should be a minimum of 3 categories and can extend to infinity. They can further be of two types:

  • *Nominal Categorical Features:* These features' values have no relationship with each other and do not follow any specific order. For instance, encoding the types of jackets like `{bomber:1, biker:2, trucker:3, denim:4, track:5, parka:6}` is a great example where the discrete values are independent of each other.

  • *Ordinal Categorical Features:* The values of these categorical features have an order to them. An example would be encoding product sizing as `{XXS:1, XS:2, S:3, M:4, L:5, XL:6, XXL:7}` where the discrete values follow the same order as that of the product sizing, i.e., `S<M` following `3<4` and so on.

Assembling meaningful features worthy enough to contribute significant predictive power to a learning algorithm requires much effort and time. Before we dive into the different techniques like Feature Extraction, Feature Selection, and so on in the upcoming sections, it is necessary to understand the distinction between features and worthy features. The following pointers might help:

- We should avoid discrete features that rarely occur in the dataset. As a rule of thumb, we can say that a good feature value has an appearance rate of at least *1%*. Checking the distribution of feature values enables a model to learn the relationship between the feature and the label. Conversely, a rare feature adds no significant value, and the model can not make any predictions based on that feature. For instance, if there are only *0.05%* of the products having the size *XXXS*, it is better to discard those examples.

- It is preferred to have feature names such that they convey their meaning concisely. For example, if we record a user's body weight, a feature like `weight_lb` or `weight_kg` makes much more sense than a feature named `weight`.

- While doing feature engineering, it is essential to deal with discontinuities in the feature values very carefully. A meaningful floating-point feature should not contain peculiar out-of-range values. Take the ratings of a product; in that case, `user_rating=3.2` makes sense while `user_rating=-0.5` does not. The best way to overcome it would be to mark the valid values using a custom boolean flag, like `is_user_rating_defined`.

- To maintain feature stability, we should avoid using mappings from an external source as feature values. For example, it is better to have the feature `user_language='en'` and use this as an input to the model (after creating a vocabulary and transforming it), rather than using an external source that maps `'en'` to say *8* and using `user_language=8` as an input to the model.

1 • FEATURE SELECTION

As we progress on solving complex problems, we try to build advanced models and have informative features. And as the number of features increases, the amount of data required for the model to be generalizable enough for good performance also grows exponentially. This requirement increases the storage space and the processing time for the model. In this sense, the value added by an additional feature might become minuscule compared to the overhead it adds at some point. This phenomenon is referred to as the *Curse of Dimensionality*.

Even if we have sufficient data to cater to the additional dimensionality to avoid *overfitting* the model, extra features make the model heavier by requiring additional time and resources for training and serving. Therefore it is always good to keep a minimal feature space by retaining only the most impactful features. This process of selecting a subset of relevant features for use in our model is called *Feature Selection*. The key premise of opting for feature selection is that the data contains many redundant or irrelevant features that can be discarded without any information loss. Peter Norvig, a celebrated ML Scientist, has put forward the power of data and features in a compelling way: *"More data beats clever algorithms, but better data beats more data."*

Thus, feature selection helps avoid the *curse of dimensionality* and paves the way for shorter training and serving times, which ultimately translates to a better end-user experience. The resultant models are easier to interpret and reason with. We could also reason this idea with *Occam's Razor* or *The Law of Parsimony*, that we lose explainability when we have many features. By reducing the number of learnable parameters, we can also observe a reduction in the model overfitting. On the contrary, if the ratio of learnable parameters and the available data is high, the models might memorize the training data, thus hurting its generalization capability.

The selection of optimum features can be divided into two phases: a *search technique* that proposes new features and an *evaluation measure* that gauges the usefulness of those features. Usually, there are three main categories of feature selection algorithms:

1. The *filter method* uses a statistical measure to score a feature and evaluate the relationship between the feature and the label, like mutual information or correlation coefficient. Based on the measure's value, we filter out the features we need to select for our model.

2. The *wrapper method* considers the selection of a set of features as a search problem. Using the technique of *Recursive Feature Elimination (RFE)*, for example, this method evaluates multiple models by adding or removing features until we find an optimal combination that maximizes model performance.

3. The *embedded method* uses algorithms that have built-in feature selection routines as part of the model's learning. These algorithms select only those features which contribute to the performance maximally. Some examples of such algorithms are LASSO Regression and Random Forest.

Let us go through a handful of feature selection techniques commonly used in the industry and academia that provide the best results in majority use cases.

I• LASSO Regression Analysis

Least Absolute Shrinkage and Selection Operator (LASSO) is a regression analysis method that selects an optimal subset of features to increase the model's performance. It uses the *L1 Regularization*, which penalizes the absolute values of the objective function's coefficients, to restrict their values to grow too large and overfit on the data. As a result, essential features' coefficients increase in value, and irrelevant ones become zero to reduce the coefficients' absolute sum, automatically selecting essential features.

II• Principal Component Analysis

Principal Component Analysis (PCA) is a statistical approach that reduces dimensionality to increase the model's interpretability without incurring information loss. PCA transforms the data containing possibly correlated features into data with linearly uncorrelated features (also called *principal components*). The transformation is defined in such a way that the first principal component captures the maximum possible variance. Each succeeding component captures variance in decreasing order while maintaining no correlation with other components. PCA is an adaptive data analysis technique that can be easily tailored to various domains, data structures, and algorithms. It is instrumental in fighting the curse of dimensionality by selecting only those features that capture the maximum variance in the data.

III• Feature Importance Ranking

Feature Importance Ranking is a statistical approach of quantifying every feature's predictive power with respect to the label and ranking them based on the relative *importance score*. As a general rule, features that positively influence the model performance or have a high predictive power are considered more important than the rest. Understanding the features' contributions improves model interpretability and explainability.

Assessing real-world scenarios, we often have a budget for the number of features that we can not exceed due to scaling concerns. In such cases, it becomes essential to select the subset of features, from all the possible ones, that would contribute the most in delivering the best performance. Following are the three popular methods for computing feature importance scores for the features, which can then be used for feature selection:

A • REGRESSION ANALYSIS

Regression Analysis is a statistical approach to estimate the relationship between the features and the target variable. Using the regression model's parameters, we can identify which features have a relatively high impact on predicting the target variable accurately. Apart from crudely computing the importance of individual features, this method can also reveal how the features interact with each other while predicting the target variable or to say if there is a synergic effect.

In cases where we only have one feature, we can use a linear regression model to learn a straight line that best approximates the data. For instance, consider $y = b + mx$ where y is the target variable, x is the feature, and b and m are constant terms learned by the algorithm. In such cases, the value of m can quantify the strength of the relationship between y and x. We can extend this concept to multiple features, viz. $y = b + \sum m_i x_i$, where the coefficient m_i of each feature x_i represents the importance score of that feature in terms of its predictive power assuming that features have been normalized.

However, the linear regression model is only useful when the feature and the target variable are linearly related. A vital adage *"correlation is not causation"* should be kept in mind while performing regression analysis since regression analysis can not effectively convey the cause-and-effect relationship between the features and the target.

B • DECISION TREES

As a Machine Learning model, Decision Trees are sensitive to change in data since the computation is ultimately a sequence of branching operations based on comparisons of feature values with their respective thresholds. They are susceptible to high variance in predicting the target variable with even small data changes since they tend to overfit. For this reason, ensemble learning methods like *Random Forest* are preferred as they construct multiple decision trees on different splits of data, thus reducing the variance by averaging various deep decision trees. Random Forest further reduces the variance by randomly selecting subsets of features for each decision tree within.

The relative rank (or the depth) of a decision node in a tree can be used to assess the relative importance of the feature associated with the node. Since features used towards the top of the tree influence decisions for a larger fraction of the input samples, they could be considered more critical.

When we split the data into two parts based on a feature value in the decision tree, the resulting splits are more uniform and have less data impurity. The relative decrease in impurity combined with the fraction of samples handled by the decision node can act as a normalized estimate of that feature's predictive power. By averaging the estimates of predictive ability over several randomized trees, we can reduce the variance of such a measure, commonly known as the *Mean Decrease in Impurity (MDI)*, and use it for feature selection.

C• Permutation Testing

Permutation Feature Importance is a model-agnostic methodology of computing the relative importance scores. The value is quantified as the decrease in a model's performance metric (accuracy, cross-entropy, etc.) when a single feature value is shuffled randomly. Randomly shuffling the feature values (or dropping them altogether) disrupts the relationship between that particular feature and the target value. The decrease in the model performance can be attributed to that feature's predictive power and indicates how much the model depends on it. We repeat the process for every feature and compare the differences in the model performance. Conceptually an important feature leads to a more considerable decrease in model performance than other less important ones.

Permutation testing can be computationally costly, especially if the feature set is substantially huge. However, it is preferable over other model-specific techniques, like decision trees, as it can be applied to any model and focuses on the performance measure of interest.

2• Feature Correlation

While discussing feature importance ranking techniques like regression analysis, we mentioned how they helped understand the correlation between the features and the target variables. Building on that concept, *Feature Correlation* is a statistical approach to determine the correlation amongst the features themselves. It establishes the statistical association between a feature pair and the degree to which the input variables are linearly related.

A feature correlation study helps in understanding the data better. Features with high correlation do not provide added signals to the model in predicting the target variable. So, keeping only one of all the correlated features would minimally impact the model performance. This aids feature selection and eventually reduces the dimensionality of the feature space.

Furthermore, a feature correlation study can help in predicting the values of features that might be missing. For instance, we can treat the feature whose value is missing as the target variable and train a separate model to predict its value from the other correlated features. This trick has been known to boost the model performance if the missing feature is an important one.

The numerical measure of correlation that determines the strength of the input variables' relationship is known as the *Correlation Coefficient*. There are multiple ways of calculating correlation coefficients, and the most popular one is *Pearson's Product-Moment Correlation Coefficient (PPMCC)*. It quantifies the linear correlation between the two features X and Y as $\rho(X,Y) = cov(X,Y) \div \sigma_X\sigma_Y$ where $cov(X,Y)$ is the covariance between the two input variables and σ_X, σ_Y denote their standard deviations, respectively. The value of PPMCC ranges between $+1$ and -1, where $+1$ is a total positive linear correlation, 0 is no linear correlation, and -1 is a total negative linear correlation. It should be noted that PPMCC does not reflect anything about the non-linear relationship. In a pair of features, the two can be correlated in one of the following ways:

1. *Positive Correlation:* When both the features move in tandem, i.e., in the same direction of change, they are both positively correlated. The linear relationship between them is such that if one increases, the other increases too, and vice

versa. The coefficient's value indicates the degree to which one of the features changes in value relative to the other in the pair. For a positive correlation, the coefficient is greater than zero.

2. *Negative Correlation:* In this case, both features move in tandem as well, albeit in opposite directions. When one increases, the other decreases, and hence it is also known as *inverse correlation*. A coefficient value of less than zero represents a negative correlation between the feature pair.

3. *No Correlation:* A coefficient of zero indicates that there exists no linear relationship between the features. An increase or decrease in one of them does not affect the other, and hence the two are unrelated features.

3 • FEATURE IMPUTATION

There is no denying the fact that the data available for modeling, especially from real-world sources, is noisy by nature. Missing values of attributes (or features) are prevalent forms of noise. These missing values introduce a substantial amount of bias and lead to complicated data analysis. Hence, we attempt to fill in the data gaps before we proceed with analysis or modeling. This process of replacing missing values with their substitutes to achieve a sense of completeness in the data is known as *Feature Imputation.*

The missing values are often encoded as *none, null, blank, not a number (NaN),* or some predefined placeholder. As discussed, these missing values dramatically affect the data quality and thwart the model's performance. One might believe that eliminating the records with missing values would be the easiest way out. However, it leads to the loss of valuable information and also reduces the volume of the dataset. A sophisticated strategy would be to fill in the cracks using estimation techniques such that it does not disturb the inherent data representation or distribution.

Before we proceed to talk about the different imputation techniques, it is worthwhile to put forward the three types of missing values:

1. *Missing Completely At Random (MCAR)*: There is no discernable pattern in an attribute's missing values. Neither the missing values are related to some other attribute in the dataset. The probability of missing a particular data point is the same throughout the dataset, or to say, the absence of values is entirely random. An example would be a user forgetting to mention the size purchased while reviewing a product.

2. *Missing At Random (MAR)*: The missing values have a pattern or relate to other observed attributes' values. The probability of missing a particular data point is the same only within groups defined by the non-missing or observed data. For example, it is highly probable for women users to skip adding body weight in a product review or their profile compared to their male counterparts.

3. *Missing Not At Random (MNAR)*: The probability of missing a particular data point can not be determined or remains unknown. It is one of the most complex of all since it could be due to an external glitch or be time-sensitive in nature. Consider a technical error that led to the user rating field not rendering in the UI. For that reason, all the product reviews had no ratings associated with them for quite some time. These chunks of missing values, all belonging to a particular product or gathered in the same week perhaps, can not be attributed as random missing data.

Now let us discuss some imputation techniques to improve the quality of input data:

- **Statistical Imputation:** This method involves computing statistical measures like the mean or the median of the observed values and then using these to substitute the missing values. It is essential to compute these statistical measures separately for each attribute since the values' scales or ranges might differ. Though it is a straightforward and clean way to impute missing values, it can only be used for numerical data. It gives poor results when used on categorical or binary features values for obvious reasons. Since it does not take into account data correlation, it does not lead to high accuracy imputation. Another variation of this technique is to use the most frequently occurring value to substitute. This trick works better for categorical features though it introduces a bias in the data and disrupts data distribution. For numerical data, this can also be done by simply substituting with a zero or a predefined constant value, which might or might not be the most-frequent occurring.

• *Hot-Deck Imputation:* This is a common imputation method that randomly selects a *similar* data record *closest* to the current record and replaces the missing values with the observed values in the selected record.

• *Cold-Deck Imputation:* This method uses an entirely different dataset closest to the current one in essence and uses its attributes to fill in the missing values. This method is not at all preferred since it leads to erroneous results.

• *Regression Imputation:* A regression model is deployed treating the attribute with missing values as target variables and remaining attributes as features. Using the non-missing values for training, we can use the predicted values to fill in the gaps. This method has an added advantage over statistical imputation since it considers feature correlation. The simple regression method tries to follow the general trend and fits the best line but does not introduce an error term in the imputed values. For this reason, *Stochastic Regression Imputation* is used, which adds the average regression variance to the regression imputations to introduce error in the imputed value.

- **k-Nearest Neighbours (k-NN) Imputation:** This method uses the feature similarity concept to predict the missing values using the non-missing data records. It finds k nearest neighbors to the data record in consideration and imputes the value based on the k-NN methodology. It is usually more accurate than the statistical imputation technique but is computationally expensive. It also does not react well to data with outliers.

- **Deep Neural Network (DNN) Imputation:** One of the most precise techniques, which works well for both categorical and numerical features, uses deep neural networks. A DNN is trained on non-missing values, and the predicted values are served as imputation values for missing attributes. It is very accurate compared to other techniques discussed above but can be computationally expensive for massive datasets.

Despite discussing multiple imputation techniques, we can not determine the best one. Each methodology is suitably crafted for different requirements. Based on the use case, missing attributes' data types, and the dataset in question, we often have to experiment until we find the best-suited strategy.

4• FEATURE INTERACTION

Feature Interaction is an effective process that provides a quick way to engineer features on top of the existing ones. To understand this clearly, consider a dataset that primitively has only two features $F1$ and $F2$. We can decompose the prediction function into the following terms: the bias, $F1$'s coefficient, $F2$'s coefficient, and $(F1 \times F2)$'s coefficient. The last one represents the interaction quotient between the two features. The interaction between two features can be defined as the change in the prediction function's result by varying the features after considering the individual feature effects. If the prediction function can be decomposed as the aggregate of the two individual features, we can assume the interaction between them to be *null*.

The concept can be generalized to a dataset with n different features, where the interaction could occur between all n features or less. In such cases, we can produce $^nC_2$ interaction features of degree 2, $^nC_3$ interaction features of degree 3, and so on. Though this process helps generate more features in the dataset with low effort, we have to choose the maximum *degree of interaction* carefully. A higher degree of interaction would probably lead to significantly more features, which could lead to overfitting of the model if the data is not enough, viz. the *curse of dimensionality*.

Friedman's H-Statistic is a popular measure to compute the strength of the interaction. This statistic is essentially dimensionless and typically takes on values between 0 to 1. Friedman's H-Statistic value of 0 signifies that the interaction term has no predictive power, whereas value of 1 means the interaction term is solely responsible for predicting. Having a value greater than one is also possible and very difficult to interpret. It happens when the interaction term's variance is much larger than the variance of the two features' individual effects. We can use Friedman's H-Statistic to our advantage by employing it to avoid the curse of dimensionality. To craftily select features from a large set, we can pick only the ones with high impact interaction levels and drop the ones below a threshold.

However, calculating the Friedman's H-Statistic is a computationally expensive process since it involves estimating individual features' marginal distributions without the interaction term. Since these estimates come with their variance as well, the results are highly unstable. Furthermore, this statistic methodology functions well under the assumption that the features can all be shuffled independently, or there is no correlation. Thus in the case where the correlation coefficient is high, the assumption gets violated, and Friedman's H-Statistic leads to invalid results. It is worth noting that this technique does not gel well with pixels as inputs, so we should avoid this in problems involving images as data. Alternatives to Friedman's H-Statistic for quantifying feature interactions include *Variable Interaction Networks (VIN)* and *Greenwell Partial Dependence Functions*.

5 • FEATURE VISUALIZATION

So far, it is crystal clear that features play an influential part in Machine Learning model's performance. Thus, it is valuable to comprehend how input features influence the model's outcome to enhance model interpretability and guide future iterations for model improvement and scaling. Computing feature importances and interaction scores help identify crucial features; however, if we want to dive deeper into how those features impact the model outcomes, we can use visualization methodologies. *Feature Visualization* is an approach that we apply to emphasize the learning path of features in a model and make it more interpretable.

Feature Visualization techniques are typically used with neural networks to understand their working better. *Deep Neural Networks (DNNs)* are known to have the ability to learn high-level features in the hidden layers, which reduces the feature engineering load quite a lot. However, their opacity reduces the model's explainability. The numerous transformations in that black box of hidden layers are a secret until we get an output. Thus, feature visualization aims to discover key inputs that relate to specific outcomes and visually inspect them.

For a unit of a DNN, feature visualization can be performed by detecting the input that maximizes the activation of a unit. The unit could be a neuron, a complete layer, or even the final prediction. There could be millions of neurons in a DNN; therefore, visualizing for each one of them is cumbersome and a time-consuming process. To optimize that, we instead use bigger units for visualization, for instance, activation maps. In specific cases, like *Convolutional Neural Networks (CNNs or ConvNets)*, which are majorly used in image recognition tasks, the unit could even refer to a feature map extracted from the raw image. After training the ConvNet, we can feed it specific images to predict and visualize the feature mapping's heatmap. The heatmap might indicate what type of features each particular unit is learning, thus providing more insights into the network's decision.

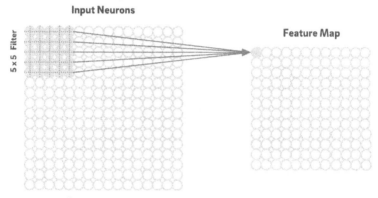

A visualization of a 5x5 filter convolving around a 16x16 input and producing a 12x12 activation (or feature) map.

Another exciting way to visualize the features, specifically the ones that improve the neural network's predictive performance, is to introduce an *attention layer* in the network. The idea is similar to computing importance scores of the features. However, unlike feature importance ranking, which generically ranks the features for the entire prediction task, the attention layer captures the contextual importance. Essentially, attention layers highlight (or give more weight) to the features that would positively influence a particular output's prediction. By further visualizing the outputs of these attention layers, we better understand the neural network's working. The addition of attention layers has proven useful for *Recurrent Neural Networks (RNNs)* the most. The structure of RNNs allows it to capture temporal dynamic context for tasks like speech recognition. The attention layers help it focus on storing the essential parts, thus improving its performance.

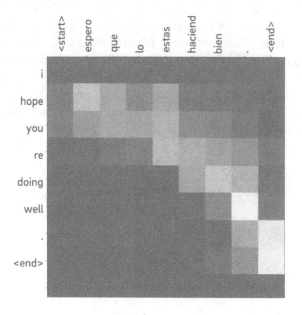

Based on a sequence-to-sequence model for Spanish to English translation, this heat map shows which parts of the input sentence have the model's attention while translating.

There is currently active research in the domain of neural feature visualization with various optimization and attribution objectives. It has become one of the most promising techniques for understanding neuron interactions, activation mechanisms, thus enhancing interpretability. As a stand-alone process, it might not yield satisfactory explanations; however, if used as a building block synergistically with other model interpretability tools, it empowers humans to uncover these complex networks' functioning.

6 • FEATURE AUTOMATION

So far, we discussed varied processes involved in engineering features for a model to improve its performance and interpretability. This study has made it clear that typically feature engineering is a drawn-out manual affair. It relies heavily on domain knowledge, intuitive exploration, data analysis, and manipulation. With multiple such components, this process can be too cumbersome and time-consuming, despite which the eventual feature set is limited by individual subjectivity, imagination, and time.

We can overcome this manual process by opting for automated feature engineering techniques to accelerate feature generation and experimentation. *Feature Automation* is a technique that generates all the possible candidate features from the given dataset from which the best could be filtered out and used for model training. The automatically generated feature set might be huge and not always optimal, but it provides us with an input feature set that generates good baseline metrics. Using domain knowledge, intuitive exploration, and the techniques discussed in this chapter for feature selection, we can improve this feature set further.

As the volume of datasets increase, it is becoming crucial to extract as much information as possible to create an effective solution. In one of their well-liked articles titled *A Few Useful Things to Know about Machine Learning*, Pedro Domingos has stated an exciting take on feature automation: *"One of the holy grails of machine learning is to automate more and more of the feature engineering process."*

A popular tool in use these days for feature automation is *Featuretools*. It is an open-source Python framework that automatically creates features, even from temporal and relational datasets. It works on the principle of *Deep Feature Synthesis (DFS)* that stacks the *primitives* on the feature directly extracted from the dataset to fabricate complex ones. Primitives can be considered the fundamental units of Featuretools, defined as the individual computations that can be applied singularly or in conjugation with others. Examples of primitives could be *aggregates* like mean, sum, average, or transforms. Applying combined primitives leads to a more descriptive feature. These descriptive features have more *'depth'*, which increases each time we clamp an additional primitive. These complex descriptive features have proven to extract intricate patterns from the data more effectively and assist in model training.

Despite being recently developed, automated feature engineering is gaining much traction these days. It has helped improve the standard error-prone workflow by cutting down the time spent on brainstorming and experimentation, delivering interpretable feature sets, and fixing data leakage issues up to quite an extent by filtering time-dependent data. Despite still being developed, this methodology is already providing significant gains, thus enabling Machine Learning modelers in multiple domains to use the baked-in knowledge regarding the data without expending a sizable quota of time, effort, and money.

CHAPTER 5

MACHINE LEARNING ALGORITHMIC APPLICATION

So far, we have secured the ability to create datasets from multiple web sources and learned various techniques to process the data to construct features for fueling the machine learning models. To strengthen our knowledge more, we shall now study different paradigms of Machine Learning. This chapter focuses on identifying well-suited algorithms for solving challenging problems with respect to the dataset we created. The aim is to provide a basic understanding of algorithms in terms of their data requirement and not discuss nitty-gritty details that are already available from other sources.

1 • MACHINE LEARNING PARADIGM IDENTIFICATION

Despite having diverse realms of Machine Learning applications, the high-level overview of the workflow remains the same. The standard steps include the following:

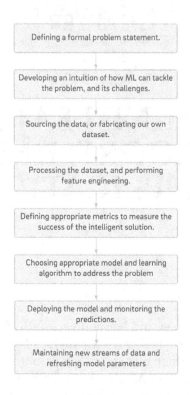

Defining a formal problem statement.

Developing an intuition of how ML can tackle the problem, and its challenges.

Sourcing the data, or fabricating our own dataset.

Processing the dataset, and performing feature engineering.

Defining appropriate metrics to measure the success of the intelligent solution.

Choosing appropriate model and learning algorithm to address the problem

Deploying the model and monitoring the predictions.

Maintaining new streams of data and refreshing model parameters

A high-level workflow of Machine Learning application.

Comprehensively understanding this workflow points out that the ideation and problem definition steps are separated from the actual Machine Learning application and deployment steps by the ones encompassing data sourcing and preprocessing. This flow indicates that applying a specific algorithm to *learn* the Machine Learning model's parameters leans on the nature and volume of data we possess. By learning, we refer to a model's capability to retain knowledge from *past experiences* (via the training data provided) and put that to use for *new unseen experiences* (i.e., test data).

We will begin this section by examining the three Machine Learning paradigms: *Supervised Learning, Unsupervised Learning,* and *Reinforcement Learning*. These three paradigms are a high-level categorization of the various techniques we have at our disposal today. We would also illustrate how we can map the quality datasets we collected to each of the paradigms to address the prediction problems.

I• SUPERVISED LEARNING

Supervised Learning is one of the most widely applied Machine Learning paradigms. In the Supervised Learning paradigm, we have a set of input-output pairs (in the form of a *labeled training dataset*), and the task is to learn a mapping function to predict the output of the *unseen* input (i.e., the ones not present in the training dataset) as accurately as possible. It is aptly named, as the algorithm has the *labeled training dataset* to observe and learn the mapping function from, just as a *supervisor*.

In simple mathematical terms, let us assume we have a labeled training dataset that represents the input variables by X and the label by Y. We have a function f that provides a mapping between the two, i.e., $f(X) = Y$. Our goal is to learn the mapping function f, such that on any given unseen example X' we can compute its label Y' with utmost accuracy. There are primarily two different techniques of Supervised Learning viz. *Classification* and *Regression,* and we will be discussing them later in this chapter.

This type of learning paradigm gels well with our *Guided Dataset Search* philosophy, which we discussed previously while learning how to gather data for a defined problem. In that instance, we had a north-star in terms of the problem statement and the essential data signals. The search consisted of finding relevant input-output pairs where we could easily apply a Supervised Learning technique. Let us consider the *Clothing Fit* dataset we have been working with for the *Size Recommendation* problem. We have the input as to what sizes of products customers have purchased, how it fits, and other details of products and customers' measurements. Our task is to learn the mapping function such that in the future, we can recommend the sizes of a product a user should purchase for a good fit.

However, we need to make a mental note that the dataset we have gathered from external sources will not directly address the Supervised Learning problem. For instance, in the *Size Recommendation* problem, the ideal dataset should have information about what size of a product best fits the user compared to all the different sizes available. But in reality, the customers only try 1-2 sizes of a given product. They cannot review the whole catalog of sizes available.

In cases like these, we need to alter our problem definition. The updated statement should approximate the original problem and gel well with the dataset gathered. Applying this principle to the *Size Recommendation* problem, we can calibrate it as a *Size Fit* problem instead. We have an input pair of *user profile* (i.e., UserID and body measurements) and *product size* purchased. The goal is to learn which size of the product would best fit that potential customer. Once we can reliably and accurately predict the fit of the catalog sizes of products on the users, we can infer the perfect size to recommend to the customers. In actuality, we recommend the catalog size having the highest probability of being the best fit for a particular user.

II • UNSUPERVISED LEARNING

Unsupervised Learning is the type of Machine Learning paradigm that does not require labeled data points. Theory projects them to be intelligent enough to look for patterns without human supervision in the provided data with *no* labels. Unsupervised Learning usually tends to be a goal in itself, where finding patterns in the data is the objective. Since we give no hints regarding the patterns we are looking for, the algorithm methodizes itself. It comes up with rules to marshal the data and discover patterns. There are primarily two different techniques of Unsupervised Learning viz. *Clustering* and *Association*, and we will be discussing them later in this chapter.

This type of learning paradigm gels well with our *Unguided Dataset Search* philosophy, which we discussed previously while learning how to gather data without any objective in mind. Since the intuition about what problems these datasets serve well is sufficient, we focus on gathering as much information as possible to help the algorithm detect patterns efficiently.

Let us consider the *News Category* dataset. It contains details like news category, news headlines, a short description of news stories, publication date, author, etc. From a first glance, we can use this dataset to predict news categories given the headlines, serving a simple example for Supervised Learning. This dataset's more exciting use would be to identify news-worthy themes within each category, like *entertainment, politics, fashion,* etc. If we observe, we do not have any labels about news-worthiness or common themes across the headlines. Hence, discovering those patterns from the data is the Unsupervised Learning algorithm's job.

An elementary approach to detect common themes across headlines would be to use *Topic Modeling* on each category's headline text. Topic Modeling is a popular learning technique, especially in natural language processing tasks. It scans the set of text documents provided, extracts similar word and phrase patterns within them, and then automatically learns to cluster word groupings and similar expressions that best characterize the given set of text documents. Using this statistical model to discover abstract themes in our data furthers our understanding of what makes it to the news article, thus identifying newsworthy stories in the future.

Semi-Supervised Learning

In contemporary times, there are cases where a small quota of labeled data is integrated with a large quantity of unlabeled data to increase the learning accuracy. This type of learning is often referred to as *Semi-Supervised Learning* since it falls between Supervised Learning and Unsupervised Learning.

A simple example could be where we have a large set of articles, imagine all the content present on the internet, and we need to categorize them without actually providing the categories. We could start with a minimal quantity of labeled articles and let the algorithm learn to categorize the rest. This method works since manually categorizing all the data could be very expensive, but unlabeled data is inexpensive to source. The algorithm can be free to construct new categories in some cases. This technique of self-training comes in handy to categorize and also rank those articles. Another typical example of Semi-Supervised Learning is speech analysis since labeling every part of multiple audio files is too cumbersome.

Since this learning paradigm is a combination of both Supervised and Unsupervised Learning, it has characteristics of both under the following assumptions:

- *Continuity Assumption*: Amongst the data points

provided, the ones closer to each other map to a similar label.

- *Cluster Assumption*: We can group all the data points provided on specific criteria and the ones in the same group map to the same label.

III • REINFORCEMENT LEARNING

Reinforcement Learning is the type of Machine Learning paradigm where the algorithm learns how to take a sequence of decisions in an uncertain environment. The objective is to maximize the cumulative reward gained by making a series of decisions. Imagine facing a game-like situation where each action either gets us a reward or a penalty, but we are not aware of them beforehand. The goal of the game is to maximize the total reward at the end. Since we do not have any hint regarding optimally playing the game, we would initially play via a trial-and-error approach and gather information about the reward policy. Then we would use that information to guide our following decisions, trying to maximize the rewards.

Similarly, a Reinforcement Learning model learns how to perform the task, starting with simple random trials and tuning its parameters based on the received reward. As the model parameters converge, the model gets more sophisticated and can perform the said task more optimally. We compare this paradigm to how human intelligence works, and if provided enough computational resources, Reinforcement Learning can consolidate experiences from a multitude of parallel gameplays. It can leverage the power of search and come up with a trailblazing algorithm within a short period.

This paradigm is different from Supervised Learning because it does not require a labeled dataset of input-output pairs.

Instead, it uses function approximation to tie the current state with the next action. It strikes a balance between exploring the uncharted territories and exploiting the knowledge gained so far to develop a strategy that maximizes rewards in the long term. A simple example of this learning paradigm could be *Autonomous Driving*. Since we can not know of every situation that could occur on the road while driving, we can not provide a labeled dataset. Based on the external factors of road condition, traffic, or weather, our goal is to minimize ride time, maximize speed within the limit, and reach the destination safely without causing an accident.

Reinforcement Learning might seem more intuitive than other paradigms, yet there are some striking caveats attached to it:

- Data collection for this paradigm is not straightforward; we have to rely on running simulations for that.

- Designing the reward is a challenge in itself, and it can have unseen consequences if done frivolously. For example, the reward of minimizing the traveling time for autonomous vehicles could be very dangerous without appropriate constraints like speed limit, direction, and so on.

- Reinforcement Learning can maximize long-term rewards efficiently; however, the algorithm's immediate decision might not be intuitive.

- It could be challenging to measure worst-case performance since collecting data in a standard form for such scenarios might not be possible.

2 • DEEP DIVE: SUPERVISED LEARNING TECHNIQUES & THEIR APPLICATIONS

As discussed previously, Supervised Learning techniques are designed to learn by example. Typically, new Machine Learning practitioners kick off their journey by experimenting with different varieties of Supervised Learning techniques. Let us dive deep into the two fundamental techniques of Supervised Learning viz. *Classification* and *Regression*.

I • CLASSIFICATION

Classification is a popular Supervised Learning approach where the machine learns to map data to one of the N defined labels from the training dataset. It then uses this knowledge to classify the new unseen data points (referred to as the test dataset) as accurately as possible. Usually, the N categories defined in the training dataset are independent of each other. The algorithm is not expected to categorize the test data in categories other than the N defined ones. A simple example could be classifying a tumor in the human body as malignant or benign using the body scan images and other features like size, color, growth speed, etc. This predictive modeling technique is further broadly classified as follows:

> **1. Binary Classification:** These tasks require the algorithm to categorize a data record into one of the two classes, like *yes/no, malignant/benign, spam/not spam, sarcastic/non-sarcastic*, etc.
>
> **2. Multi-Class Classification:** These tasks train and expect the algorithm to classify into one of the many possible classes, for example, *primary colors: red/blue/yellow, fruits: orange/apple/peach/guava*, and so on.

It is noteworthy that modeling techniques designed for

binary classification tasks can also be applied to multi-class classification problems. There are simple heuristics that split the multi-class classification problem into multiple binary classification tasks. Two such heuristics are:

- *One-Vs-Rest (OVR)*: OVR is also referred to as the *One-Vs-All (OVA)* approach. This heuristic picks up a class and trains a model to differentiate the picked class from all the remaining classes. We do this repeatedly until we have multiple models that learn to assign a probability score to each class. For example, let us consider a task to classify a color swatch into one of the colors *Red/Blue/ Yellow/Green*. We will be training four binary classification models viz. *Model 1*: Red vs. (Blue or Yellow or Green), *Model 2*: Blue vs. (Yellow or Green or Red), *Model 3*: Yellow vs. (Green or Red or Blue), and *Model 4*: Green vs. (Red or Blue or Yellow). Undoubtedly, this becomes cumbersome when we have many categories, a large dataset, or when the model is too complex to train multiple times.

- *One-vs-One (OVO)*: This heuristic picks up different pairs of classes and trains a binary classification model for each till we learn how to assign a probability score for each category. Using the same example as above, except, in this case, we will have six different models, viz. *Model 1*: Red vs. Blue, *Model 2*: Red vs. Yellow, *Model 3*: Red vs. Green, *Model 4*: Blue vs. Yellow, *Model 5*: Blue vs. Green, *Model 6*: Yellow vs. Green.

Now, let us discuss some popular classification techniques, specifically for binary classification tasks.

A • LOGISTIC REGRESSION

Logistic Regression is based on the statistical logit model used to model a particular event's probability using prior experiences. It is the go-to algorithm for binary classification to model the relationship between the binary response variable (i.e., either of the two outcome classes) and the set of predictor variables, i.e., features from the data. During the inference time, the algorithm calculates the data record's probability of being associated with each class and assigns it to the class with the highest probability of occurrence. If the likelihood of one of the two classes is p, where p lies between 0 and 1, the likelihood of the other class would be $1-p$.

Some common examples where logistic regression algorithm comes in handy are:

- Classify an incoming mail as spam or not: *Spam: 1, Not Spam: 0*

- Classify a tumor as malignant or benign; *Malignant: 1, Benign: 0*

- Classify a transaction as fraudulent or not; *Fraud: 1, Standard: 0*

This algorithm has the term regression in its name since the output value is derived using a linear function of the input variables (i.e., features), just like linear regression (more on this later in this section). The difference here is that we further pass this linear function of features through a logit function that squishes its value in the 0 to 1 range, representing the probability of occurrence of a class. The algorithm learns the weights or the regression equation's coefficient by maximizing the likelihood of the observed classes' occurrence.

One of the most significant advantages of this technique is its ease of implementation and training efficiency with decent model performance. Along with the actual label's probabilities, we also get conditional probabilities to use for other purposes. However, being a linear model, it does not work well when the classification boundaries are non-linear. Logistic regression algorithms are also known to not work with imbalanced classes and data with outliers. Hence, it is necessary to explore and balance the data well before proceeding with this algorithm's application.

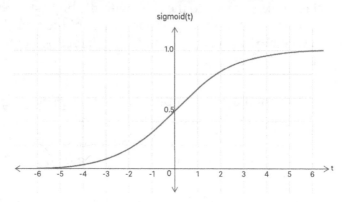

Sigmoid Activation Function.

B• Decision Trees

Decision Trees use a flowchart-like structure to help visualize decision points and their outcomes effectively. Each node in the tree represents a decision taken on a particular feature based on some thresholds, which splits the data into two or more homogeneous sets. Growing this tree involves deciding on which features to choose and what conditions to use for splitting. This process is repeated until we reach the desired stop criterion. Then, the leaves of the tree can be used to make accurate classifications. Upon completion, the entire path from the root to any of the leaf nodes indicates the different classification rules.

The decision tree's objective is to learn what features to split on and decide the respective thresholds. After this, when an unseen data record (from the test dataset) is observed, it is passed through the tree's different decision points. The final class membership is decided based on the majority vote from the data points associated with the leaf node where the unseen data record ends up. Simple examples where a decision tree can be useful could be:

- Given a pet's picture, we need to classify whether it is a *cat* or a *dog*.

- Based on a questionnaire about a person's characteristics, we need to classify them as a *gamer* or *non-gamer*.

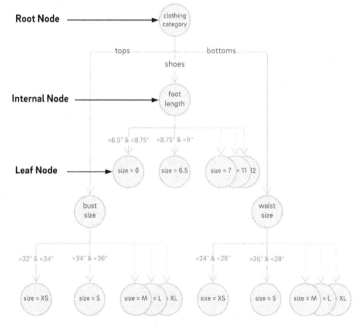

A simple decision tree for the *Size Recommendation* problem in action.

Decision Trees are intuitive and interpretable owing to their strong visualization aspect. They yield decent classification performance with not many high-end computational requirements. They also work effectively for non-linear classification boundaries. Decision Trees have proven to address class imbalance and outliers fittingly.

However, they tend to overfit if they grow without proper supervision and are not pruned carefully. Furthermore, this approach only produces the class prediction and not the probability score that is often used for ranking purposes. Regardless, Decision Tree classifiers' inductive approach for classification makes them a popular tool for Machine Learning and operations research for strategic decision analysis.

C• K-Nearest Neighbour (KNN)

k-Nearest Neighbour is a simple and easy to implement Supervised Classification technique. Like the saying *"birds of a feather, flock together"*, kNN works on the principle of proximity and assumes that data points closer to each other are similar. This classification technique finds k data points in the training data closest to the unseen data point during inference time and assigns it to the class shared by the majority of those k data points. To define the closeness, we could choose any distance metric quantifying the proximity of two data points. For categorical variables, we can use the *Hamming Distance,* which computes the number of positions at which the two variables of equal dimensions differ at corresponding positions. In the case of continuous variables, here are some standard distance measures:

- *Euclidean Distance*: It is a measure that computes the length of a straight line between two points in Euclidean space. Mathematically, it is the square root of the sum of the squares of the differences of the coordinates.

$$d(\mathbf{p}, \mathbf{q}) = d(\mathbf{q}, \mathbf{p}) = \sqrt{(q_1 - p_1)^2 + (q_2 - p_2)^2 + \ldots + (q_n - p_n)^2}$$

$$= \sqrt{\sum_{i=1}^{N} (q_i - p_i)^2}$$

- *Manhattan Distance*: It is the distance between two points measured along the axes at right angles. Mathematically, it is the sum of the absolute values of the differences of the coordinates.

$$d_1(\mathbf{p}, \mathbf{q}) = ||\mathbf{p} - \mathbf{q}||_1 = \sum_{i=1}^{N} |p_i - q_i|$$

- *Minkowski Distance*: We can consider this distance as a generalization of both the Euclidean distance and the Manhattan distance in the normed vector space. The case where $z = 1$ is equivalent to the Manhattan distance, and the case where $z = 2$ is equivalent to the Euclidean distance.

$$d(\mathbf{p}, \mathbf{q}) = \left(\sum_{i=1}^{N} |p_i - q_i|^z \right)^{\frac{1}{z}}$$

k-Nearest Neighbor is a non-parametric method. It does not make any assumptions regarding the training data's underlying data distribution, i.e., whether their classification boundaries are linear, quadratic, etc. The performance of kNN depends on the data representation and the distance measure described above. The value of k also plays a vital role. Choosing the optimal value is best done by experimentation, a process referred to as *parameter tuning*. Computing many neighbors for each data point is computationally expensive, whereas having fewer neighbors makes the model very noisy. Ideally, we choose the value of k via cross-validation by using an independent dataset other than train and test ones.

One of the plus points of kNN is its robustness to the labels' noise since the k nearest neighbors influence its decision, thereby averaging out the noise (if any). kNN does not have an explicit training phase and computes the neighbors by iterating over the test data points; hence it is aptly termed a *lazy algorithm*. But this characteristic, however, leads to longer prediction times. Another drawback of kNN is its inability to perform well on imbalanced data. In that case, it would compute neighbors closer to the majority classes only, leaving out the minority classes as outliers. kNN also suffers from the curse of dimensionality, a concept we discussed previously. As the data points' dimensions increase, we would require more data for kNN to have a decent performance.

Considering all the positives and the negatives of this easy-to-understand approach, kNN is widely used for economic forecasting, data compression, and genetic studies.

II• REGRESSION

Regression is a Supervised Learning approach where we predict a real output value based on the input features. The regression technique learns a function to model the relationship between the target value, which is continuous, and the features from training data. It then uses this knowledge to predict the output value of the unseen data points. A simple example of where a regression algorithm is useful would be predicting a taxi ride's fare where the price depends on inputs like origin, destination, duration, time, traffic, city, car type, passenger count, and so on. Let us discuss some popular Regression Algorithms.

A• LINEAR REGRESSION

Linear Regression is one of the most effortless regression techniques. We model the relationship between the scalar output (or the target variable denoted by y) and the input predictor variables (referred to as features and denoted by X) by fitting a linear function on the training dataset: $y = f(X) = b + mX$. The term b incorporates the *degree of freedom* and is called the *bias term* or *intercept*. It allows the straight line to be moved up or down in the coordinate space. Linear Regression is also referred to as the *Ordinary Least-Squares Regression* because of the way the model parameters, b and m, are learned. We minimize the sum of the squares of the vertical deviations from each data point to the straight line that best fits all the train data points.

Additionally, the learned model parameters m can also explain the strength of the relationship between the target variable and the features. This process is known as *Regression Analysis,* and we also discussed it as one of the methods for computing *Feature Importance.* That is to say, the feature with a higher model parameter value has more predictive power than the one with a lower value. We can safely remove a feature with a zero coefficient since it would not influence the model's prediction. This concept is often used in the different *regularization methods,* which puts pressure on the large values of coefficients to reduce the model's complexity. The two most common methods of regularization are:

> **1. Lasso Regularization:** This method not only focuses on minimizing the mean squared error but also on minimizing the absolute sum of the coefficients. It is also referred to as the *L1 Regularization.*

> **2. Ridge Regularization:** Apart from minimizing the mean squared error, this also minimizes the squared sum of the coefficients. It is also referred to as the *L2 Regularization.*

Linear Regression is a powerful statistical model and has wide adoption in business as it helps to find trends in customer behavior, forecasting sales, risk analysis, and so on. Based on our use case, we could have a different number of features or requirements of the regression equation, which leads us to the following types of Linear Regressions:

1. Simple Linear Regression: This is the type of approach which contains only one feature. It uses the linear equation's traditional slope-intercept form. It is denoted as the following in mathematical terms: $y = mx + b$.

2. Multivariate Linear Regression: When we have more than one feature, which is usually the case, we use this approach. In this situation, we will have multiple model parameters or the coefficient corresponding to the features. It is denoted as: $y = b + m_1x_1 + m_2x_2 + \ldots + m_nx_n$.

3. Polynomial Linear Regression: A slightly more complex regression, it is used when we have multiple features. The relationship between the target and the input variables is modeled as the qth degree polynomial, where q could be any number. For example: $y = b + m_1x_1^2 + m_2x_2^4 + \ldots + m_nx_n^q$. It remains a linear regression in the sense that the values for different features (despite being in a polynomial form) are combined linearly.

The main reason for the popularity of various Linear Regression approaches is the ease to understand and implement. The space complexity is low since saving the coefficients (also called *weights*) at the end of the training phase is the only place we use memory. With the help of regularization techniques discussed above, linear regression can perform the feature selection tasks well. This capability results in reduced dimensionality and thus helps in avoiding overfitting.

There are certain limitations of Linear Regression, which we should be mindful of when selecting this algorithm. Linear Regression works on the assumption that the data we are working with follows a *Gaussian Distribution* (or a *Normal Distribution*), which might not always be accurate. It also assumes that the relationship between the features and the target is linear. Furthermore, since linear regression tries to fit data to a single straight line, it is susceptible to noise and does not work well with outliers. We can mitigate some of these limitations by performing necessary data transformations, as discussed in the previous chapter.

B • NEURAL NETWORK

Neural Networks are modeled loosely on the working of a human brain. These biologically inspired Machine Learning models are designed to recognize patterns just like a human brain does by interpreting sensory data. A Neural Network consists of thousands of simple interconnected processing units referred to as the *neurons*. Usually, these neurons are arranged in different *layers*, and each layer feeds the data forward to the other layers. Additionally, each layer applies non-linear transformations on the data, which allow neural networks to model non-linear relationships between the features and the target variable. These transformations are applied using *activation functions*, which normalize neurons' output to a range, usually in (-1, 1) or (0,1). Some examples of activation functions include *Sinusoid, Gaussian, Rectified Linear Unit* (ReLU), *Exponential Linear Unit* (ELU), and so on. Once we reach the last layer of the Neural Network, the transformed data is responsible for giving the output of our prediction problem.

The learning aspects in Neural Networks come from parameters called *weights* that denote the strength of connections between different neurons. We randomly initialize these weights since we have limited or no knowledge at the beginning. During the training phase, we do one full pass of the Neural Network for each input from the training data. In that pass, we fuse the input data with corresponding weights, usually by multiplying, and pass them through a *non-linear activation function*. The output from this is then carried further into the Neural Network until we reach the last layer responsible for prediction. If the predicted outcome is not accurate, each neuron's weight is tuned based on a technique called *Backpropagation*. Backpropagation is a technique that allows us to effectively attribute the inaccuracy of a Neural Network's output to each neuron. Once that is done, we optimize these weights by applying iterative optimization algorithms like *Gradient Descent, AdaGrad, Adam,* etc.

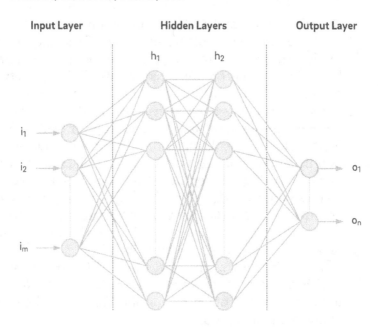

A typical *Deep Neural Network (DNN)* architecture.

One of the main advantages of Neural Networks is learning complex relationships on their own given input features and target variables. This learning is possible due to the application of non-linear transformations to the data. Research has consistently shown that simply providing more data to the network, whether new or augmented original data, rapidly improves the model performance.

However, along with more data, they also require powerful resources to train and tune the model parameters, which becomes a challenging aspect of using this technique. Hence, simpler Machine Learning algorithms outperform the intensive Neural Networks for tasks with relatively smaller available datasets. Furthermore, with an increased number of neurons and interconnections, model parameters sometimes become difficult to interpret and understand.

The primitive category of Neural Networks was *shallow*, i.e., only had an input layer and an output layer, or seldom had a single hidden layer. However, newer Neural Networks are complex and *deep*, containing multiple hidden layers of varying sizes. The application of deep Neural Networks is referred to as *Deep Learning* in today's times. Owing to Neural Networks' capability to accurately model non-linear processes, they have found applications in many disciplines, including medical diagnosis, face recognition, game playing, etc.

3 • DEEP DIVE: UNSUPERVISED LEARNING TECHNIQUES & THEIR APPLICATIONS

Based on our previous discussions, Unsupervised Learning algorithms infer patterns in the data without any prior knowledge of labels or outcomes. These algorithms help understand the data's structure by extracting patterns. In the following sections, we would be discussing the two fundamental techniques of Unsupervised Learning: *Clustering* and *Association*.

I• CLUSTERING

Clustering is one of the most popular Unsupervised Learning techniques and involves automatically discovering natural grouping in data. This approach involves grouping data points so that objects in a group (or *cluster*) are similar, while those not in the same cluster are distinctly dissimilar. The similarity and dissimilarity can be gauged based on the features associated with each data point using some metric. This statistical data analysis technique is also referred to as *Cluster Analysis*.

Clustering finds application in multiple domains involving Pattern Recognition, Information Retrieval, Image Analysis, and of course, Machine Learning (primarily Feature Engineering and Anomaly Detection). Since cluster analysis helps learn more about the problem domain, it is also a vital *knowledge discovery* tool.

There are different types of clustering algorithms, and they are defined mostly on the way they discover these dense regions of similar data points, a.k.a. the *clusters*. The identification of clusters is subjective and might require domain experience. Typically, clustering is an iterative process, where we work on the evaluation repeatedly to update the algorithm configuration until we achieve the appropriate results. Let us quickly look at some standard clustering algorithms available to us.

A• K-MEANS CLUSTERING

k-Means Clustering is a centroid-based clustering algorithm that aims to partition the data points into exactly k clusters. These k clusters are defined such that each data point belongs to the cluster with the nearest *centroid* (or the center of the cluster, which is the cluster's mean). k-Means Clustering tends to minimize the variance within the cluster based on a certain distance measure. Similar to what we discussed in the k-Nearest Neighbours technique, the distance measure for continuous variables could be Euclidean, Manhattan, or Minkowski, while for categorical, Hamming works the best.

In k-Means Clustering, we start by randomly choosing k different data points to serve as centroids. Considering the dataset has n points, we decide the remaining $n-k$ data points' membership based on the distance between them and the centroids and assign them to the closest one. Once the memberships are assigned, we compute new centroids by taking the associated points' mean and repeating the cluster assignment process. This process is repeated until the centroids stabilize, and the assignments do not change much.

k-Means Clustering is just a heuristic for an NP-hard problem and does not guarantee a globally optimum solution. Furthermore, since this algorithm starts with a random choice of centroids, different runs could yield different results; therefore, disrupting the algorithm's robustness. In any case, the accuracy and speed of k-Means Clustering depend on the data representation, the distance measure, and the value of k. Choosing the optimal value of k is best done by experimentation. k-Means Clustering algorithm is easy to understand and implement. It is usually very fast in execution and finds its applications in computer vision, vocabulary learning, image segmentation, and astronomy.

This technique's spin-off is the *k-Medians Clustering*, which uses the cluster's median as the centroid instead of the mean. This technique is more robust to outliers because of the median statistical metric but slower in execution for more massive datasets since finding the median requires sorting.

B• Gaussian Mixture Models (GMMs)

Though k-Means Clustering is one of the easiest ways to group a set of data points, it uses the naive method of assigning a cluster's centroid based on the mean value. If the mean values of two clusters are very close to each other, it becomes challenging for the k-Means Clustering to handle it, and it keeps on oscillating between the two, thus never reaching stability. The k-Means Clustering approach also fails when the shape of the clusters is not circular. Hence, to overcome the k-Means Clustering method's drawbacks, a clustering approach based on the *Expectation-Maximization (EM)* technique via *Gaussian Mixture Models (GMMs)* was fabricated.

Clustering via GMMs provides a higher level of flexibility than k-Means Clustering. It assumes the underlying data is generated from a blend of Gaussian distributions, each corresponding to a particular cluster. This assumption characterizes each cluster by a mean and a standard deviation. Thus, if we consider this in a simple 2-D coordinate space, the cluster can be elliptical and not just circular. Apart from mean and standard deviation, each cluster also has a weight parameter that determines how the corresponding Gaussian distribution is mixed with the others.

The above-mentioned assumption also means that GMMs use a *soft clustering* approach to assign the points to different clusters. This property results in *hybrid membership* of each data point, which means that a data point can belong to different clusters with varying probabilities. Initially, this degree of membership is unknown (or *latent*) and is one more element to learn to compute model parameters.

We compute various clusters' parameters using a technique called *Expectation-Maximization (EM)*. Broadly, the EM algorithm has the following steps:

1. Initialize the model parameters viz. each cluster's mean, standard deviation, and weight randomly since we have limited or no knowledge regarding the distribution.

2. *E-Step:* For each data point, using the current model parameters, estimate the degree of membership to each cluster.

3. *M-Step:* Based on the new cluster assignments as estimated in the above *E-Step*, update the model parameters.

4. Repeat the above *E-Step* and *M-Step* in order until we reach convergence.

To summarize, we are increasingly improving how much each data point belongs to each cluster at every *E-Step* and using this estimate in the *M-Step* to calculate GMM's parameters to maximize the observed data's likelihood.

For computational reasons, GMMs usually fail to work if the dimensionality of the feature space is high. They also require initial knowledge about the number of mixture models that the algorithm must try before coming to a halt. Regardless, GMMs come across as a powerful clustering technique and are more effective than the traditional clustering approaches. As an efficient tool for data analysis, GMMs have been widely applied in signal and information processing.

C• Hierarchical Clustering

Hierarchical Clustering is a technique that seeks to build a social pyramid-like structure of clusters and works well for hierarchical data like taxonomies. Strategies for Hierarchical Clustering are usually of the following two types:

Divisive Hierarchical Clustering

It is a top-down approach where we start with one giant cluster containing all the data points. We then keep splitting the cluster into two clusters (generally based on a greedy heuristic) till each data point is its own cluster.

Agglomerative Hierarchical Clustering

It is a bottom-up approach where each data point starts as an individual cluster. We then keep merging the closest clusters (with respect to the chosen distance measure) in pairs as we move up in the hierarchy. This process stops when we reach one giant cluster encompassing all the data points.

The results of Hierarchical Clustering are dendrograms with different levels of the tree representing the clusters. For instance, in Agglomerative Hierarchical Clustering, there is one root node containing all the data points, and the leaves at the bottom are data points as clusters.

Hierarchical Clustering does not require us to specify the number of clusters needed; instead, we can stop the aggregation (or division) of clusters anytime we feel we have reached the desired number of clusters. This approach is not sensitive to the distance metric we might be choosing, unlike other clustering algorithms. However, these algorithms are computationally intensive and also have large storage requirements. Despite its disadvantages, Hierarchical Clustering is an effective way of segmentation and is used in interesting cases like tracking viral outbreaks and charting evolution.

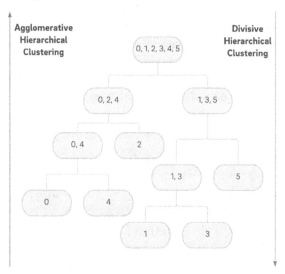

A dendrogram example of the two types of Hierarchical Clustering approaches.

II • ASSOCIATION

Another interesting approach to finding patterns without supervision involves discovering relationships between different attributes hidden in an extensive unlabeled dataset. This rule-based technique is intended to identify robust relationships in the dataset based on a well-defined measure of their *interestingness* and *significance*. For example, by analyzing customer's shopping behavior on *ModCloth*, we can pinpoint a particular set of products that a customer is highly likely to buy together. It is worth understanding that this type of association uncovers the probability of co-occurrence and does not imply causality. The order of transactions or the order of products purchased within a single transaction does not play a role in determining the rules, thus making this technique significantly different from *sequence mining*. This associative information can be used to cash in on a customer by strategically placing the distinguished products. It also helps in other marketing activities, like pricing and promotions. Apart from the above example of *market-basket analysis,* association rule learning also finds usage in malicious intrusion detection in security systems, continuous flow detection in manufacturing, and medical diagnosis via bioinformatics.

A • ASSOCIATION RULE REPRESENTATION

Relationships between various attributes in a dataset, as referred to above, are represented as association rules. An association rule is defined as an implication expression of the form: $X \Rightarrow Y$, where X and Y are disjoint sets. The set on the left-hand side is the *antecedent*. The right-hand side set is the *consequent* or the *resultant*. A simple example of an association rule in the *market-basket analysis* could be `{beanie, boots, gloves} => {sweater}`, which indicates that if the customer's cart has a *beanie, boots*, and *gloves*, they also tend to buy a *sweater*.

This small example is one of the many more intricate association rules that we can uncover from the broad set of *ModCloth's* transaction records. To put forward strong rules, we need to select the top ones from the possibilities using the following measures:

1. Support
Support measures the occurrence frequency of an attribute set, also called an *itemset* (in this case, X or Y), in the entire dataset. In mathematical terms, if itemset

X occurs in t transactions out of total T, support can be represented as:

$$support(X) = \frac{|\{t \in T; X \subseteq t\}|}{|T|}$$

2. Confidence

Confidence measures the prospect of $X \Rightarrow Y$ holding true, i.e., the probability of occurrence of Y given the occurrence of X. With respect to transactions T, the confidence value $X \Rightarrow Y$ is the proportion of transactions containing X that also include Y. Mathematically, it can be expressed as:

$$confidence(X \Rightarrow Y) = \frac{support(X \cup Y)}{support(X)}$$

3. Lift

The ratio of the observed confidence of a rule ($X \Rightarrow Y$) to the support of its consequent in a dataset is referred to as the *Lift*. We can also understand lift as essentially the rise in the probability of Y's occurrence in the cart given X's occurrence over the likelihood of Y's occurrence without any knowledge of X's occurrence. Having a greater value of the lift implies a stronger association rule. Mathematically, it can be represented as:

$$lift(X \Rightarrow Y) = \frac{confidence(X \Rightarrow Y)}{support(Y)} = \frac{support(X \cup Y)}{support(X).support(Y)}$$

4. Conviction

Conviction quantifies the ratio of the *expected* frequency of X's occurrence without Y (i.e., an incorrect prediction), assuming they are independent, and the *observed* frequency of incorrect predictions. A high conviction value means that the consequent is highly dependent on the antecedent. Having a greater value of the conviction implies a stronger association rule. Mathematically, it is expressed as:

$$conviction(X \Rightarrow Y) = \frac{1 - support(X \Rightarrow Y)}{1 - confidence(X \Rightarrow Y)}$$

Generally, the strength of an association rule is measured in terms of support and confidence values. However, other less popular measures like *leverage, collective strength*, and *all-confidence* can also be used to quantify *interestingness* and can be applied on a use case basis.

B• MINING ASSOCIATION RULES

As discussed, we create a broad set of possibilities of association rules from the given data, which are then ranked to select the robust ones based on the metrics defined above. Generating the initial set of rules and picking the top ones is referred to as the *mining association rules*.

Association rule generation is usually a two-step process:

1. Frequent Itemsets Discovery

2. Rule Formation

Usually, the step involving shortlisting of the rules is straightforward, compared to efficiently creating *itemsets* from a large dataset and selecting the frequent ones. Let us discuss this process in detail to understand better.

FREQUENT ITEMSETS DISCOVERY

The first step of mining association rules involves creating all the frequently occurring itemsets and partitioning them to form corresponding antecedents and consequents, a process referred to as the *Frequent Itemsets Discovery*. Considering there are n items in a dataset, we would find all 2^n-1 combinations via the *brute force* approach since there is no limit on the size of an itemset. The process would also involve computing the support values of all the possible combinations. We would then select the itemsets with the support value above the minimum threshold as *frequent itemsets*.

There are many efficient ways of searching the desired itemsets from the power set, exploiting the *downward closure* property of support. It ensures that for a frequent itemset, all its subsets are also frequent. Thus no infrequent itemset can be a subset of a frequent itemset. For example, this property implies that the frequency of purchase transactions of {beanie, boots} is greater than or equal to {beanie, boots, gloves}, i.e., the support value of a subset of an itemset obtained by removing one (or more) items is always greater than or equal to the original itemset. This property is also called *anti-monotonicity* and is utilized by various algorithms like *Apriori Algorithm* and *Equivalence Class Transformation (ECLAT) Algorithm*.

Apriori Algorithm

Apriori Algorithm is one of the most popular algorithms used for frequent itemset mining. It uses a *breadth-first search (BFS)* strategy to compute the Support values of itemsets. It then generates a candidate itemset exploiting the *downward closure* property of support defined above. The following are the steps involved in this algorithm:

1. Determine a threshold for the support value; we could do this via experimentation or eyeballing the requirements. This threshold value, or the minimum_support, would help prune the itemsets having the lower support value.

2. Generate all the itemsets containing only a single item where the support value is greater than or equal to the threshold.

3. Generate itemsets of size two, using combinations of the items picked in the previous steps. Then prune

all the itemsets having a support value lower than the threshold.

4. Continue this process of creating itemsets of incrementally increasing sizes from the previous steps' results, pruning them, and so on, till we reach the step that aims to build itemsets of size n.

Based on the anti-monotonicity property of support, the pruning at each step reduces the search space by a significant fraction. As the number of possible items (n) increases, this algorithm becomes computationally more efficient. The proportion is also dependent on the `minimum_support` value, which is entirely reliant on the use case. However, the Apriori Algorithm has its limitations as it requires multiple scans of the dataset at each step, thus having a high time and space complexity.

RULE FORMATION

Once the frequent itemsets are discovered, identifying association rules is a comparatively more straightforward task. The rules are formed by partitioning the frequent itemsets in a binary fashion. For instance, if `{beanie, boots, gloves, sweater}` is a frequent itemset, then the possible rules could include:

- `{beanie,boots,gloves}=>{sweater}`
- `{sweater,boots,gloves}=>{beanie}`
- `{beanie,sweater,gloves}=>{boots}`
- `{beanie,boots,sweater}=>{gloves}`
- `{boots,gloves}=>{sweater,beanie}`
- `{beanie,gloves}=>{sweater,boots}`
- `{beanie,boots}=>{sweater,gloves}`
- `{sweater,gloves}=>{beanie,boots}`

- *{sweater,boots}=>{beanie,gloves}*
- *{sweater,beanie}=>{boots,gloves}*
- *{sweater}=>{beanie,boots,gloves}*
- *{beanie}=>{sweater,boots,gloves}*
- *{boots}=>{beanie,sweater,gloves}*
- *{gloves}=>{beanie,boots,sweater}*

Out of all the possibilities, we need to pick the association rules which robustly represent a relationship. We could do this by selecting the association rules having a value of confidence above a determined threshold. Based on the anti-monotonicity property of confidence, the confidence value of rules derived from the same itemset with a larger antecedent size has a higher value than those with a larger consequent size. The reason is as the antecedent size increases, the support value decreases, and the confidence increases. To put it simply,

confidence({beanie,boots,gloves}=>{sweater})

$\geq$ *confidence({boots,gloves}=>{sweater,beanie})*

$\geq$ *confidence({beanie}=>{sweater,boots,gloves})*

Exploiting the above property, we can limit the number of rules generated and pick only the desired ones following the steps below:

1. Determine a threshold for the confidence value; we could do this via experimentation or eyeballing the requirements. This threshold value, or the *minimum_ confidence*, would be used to select the rules with a higher confidence value.

2. Starting with a frequent itemset, we shall form rules

with a single consequent and remove those having a confidence value lower than the threshold.

3. Using the rules from the previous step, we will now form rules by incrementing the number of consequents by one and applying the threshold to discard the unsatisfactory ones.

4. We repeat these steps until we have tried multiple combinations of consequents, and the number of antecedents is one.

Using the above two steps of *Frequent Itemsets Discovery* and *Rule Formation*, we can uncover well-defined association rules describing the strong relationships present in a dataset with desirable support and confidence values. To further reduce the number of association rules, specifically for business requirements, we can pick those with the highest values of lift instead. Apart from the primary type of *Association Rule Mining* discussed above, there are various other kinds like *Multi-Relation Association Rule Mining, Weighted Class Rule Mining,* and *Quantitative Association Rule Mining*, which can be applied based on the use case and the complexity of the problem.

ACKNOWLEDGMENT

The world witnessed unprecedented times in 2020, especially with the worldwide pandemic, human tragedies, and economic disruptions galore. The unfortunate series of events left earthlings in a perpetual state of fear, worry, stress, and uncertainty for an entire year, and perhaps more. Having lost all privilege of being outdoors and interacting with other human beings, we suddenly had ample time on our hands. That is when we decided to gather our thoughts, knowledge, and experiences related to the use of data in Machine Learning in the form of a book. Writing a book was indeed in both of our bucket lists, albeit never charted out. Hence, this opportunity of curating a book together on the topic we both are passionate about was the silver lining of the year for which we are eternally grateful.

The values of discipline and hard work instilled in us by our beloved families proved worthwhile, especially in this journey of writing the book and sharing with the world, all on our own. We are so thankful for their immense love, unwavering support, and steadfast encouragement to follow our dreams.

The contents of the book stem from our time at the University of California, San Diego, where we pursued our graduate studies in Computer Science specializing in Machine Learning and Artificial Intelligence. Notably, the skills demonstrated in the book are owed to the learning from the collaborative research with Dr. Julian McAuley, Dr. Mengting Wan, and Dr. Ndapa Nakashole as it was during that time the datasets mentioned were collected. A hat tip to the faculty and fellow graduate students with whom we had meaningful discussions and all those who supported us throughout our time at the graduate school.

While we write this, we also do not want to forget each other. To us, each being the pillar of strength and having faith in this book.

We both believe in a strong force that guides each one of us to our final destination. The said feat is propped up with each connection and relationship we establish in this world, which imparts us knowledge of a certain degree. With that, a heartfelt thank you to each and everyone with whom we have interacted, studied, worked, and grown up with. This one's for you!

Jigyasa Grover & Rishabh Misra

About The Author
JIGYASA GROVER

Jigyasa Grover is a Machine Learning Engineer, currently at Twitter, Inc. She has a myriad of experiences from her brief stints at Facebook, Inc., National Research Council of Canada, and Institute of Research & Development France involving Data Science, mathematical modeling, and software engineering. Having graduated from the University of California, San Diego, with a Master's degree in Computer Science with an Artificial Intelligence specialization, she is presently plying her past experiences and knowledge towards Applied Machine Learning in the online advertisements prediction and ranking domain. Red Hat 'Women in Open Source' Academic Award Winner and Google Summer of Code alumna, Jigyasa is an ardent open-source contributor as well. She served as the Director of Women Who Code and Lead of Women Techmakers for a handful of years to help bridge the gender gap in technology. In her quest to build a powerful community of girls and boys alike, and believing in *"we rise by lifting others,"* she mentors aspiring developers and Machine Learning enthusiasts in various global programs. She also has many international conference keynotes, technical talks, panels, workshops, blogs, and podcasts to her name. Apart from her technological ventures, she enjoys exploring new places, hanging out with friends and family, and has been recently having fun with baking. You can visit her online at *jigyasa-grover.github.io* or on Twitter (*@jigyasa_grover*).

About The Author

RISHABH MISRA

Rishabh Misra is a Machine Learning Engineer, currently at Twitter, Inc. He developed a passion for identifying and tackling novel and practical problems using Machine Learning during his research internships at the Indian Institute of Technology Madras, which he further explored during his Master's in Computer Science from the University of California San Diego. He combines his past engineering experiences in designing large-scale systems, working at Amazon and Arcesium (a D.E. Shaw company), and research experiences in Applied Machine Learning to develop distributed Machine Learning relevance systems. His explorations have led to several research publications in competitive ML conferences like RecSys, ACL, and WSDM. The ML community has well received the datasets collected (also used in this book) as part of his research. Kaggle recently ranked him as one of the top 20 dataset contributors, and Deeplearning.ai's "Natural Language Processing in TensorFlow" course on Coursera used his Sarcasm Detection dataset for teaching purposes. In his downtime, he enjoys watching sci-fi shows, gaming, and spending time with his family. He presently lives in San Francisco, California, and you can visit him online at *rishabhmisra.github.io* or on Twitter (@ *rishabh_misra_*).

FEEDBACK IS A GIFT

LEAVE A REVIEW

A lot of thoughtful efforts were put in the composition of the book. We would appreciate your take on it. Please share your thoughts with us and the potential readers, especially on the platform you used to access this book. In case of any other questions regarding the content of the book, feel free to reach us at *@dataform1* on Twitter or Instagram.